BRAD H. HILL

No One Is Normal

Breaking Free from Normal: Short Stories of Struggle, Adversity, and Self-Discovery

Library of Congress Control Number: 2025927216

First edition

ISBN (paperback): 979-8-9935405-2-8
ISBN (hardcover): 979-8-9935405-3-5
ISBN (digital): 979-8-9935405-4-2

This book was professionally typeset on Reedsy.
Find out more at reedsy.com

To my wife, Bonnie, my mom, and my stepdad — thank you for standing by me through both triumphs and struggles. Your love and belief in me made this book possible.

"Let go of the past, but keep the lessons it taught you."
— Chiara Gizzi

"Sometimes you don't know how strong you are until being strong is the only choice you have."
— Bob Marley

Contents

II   Bonnie's Story

III   Conclusion

Foreword

Brad and I met in 7th grade — the "meh" year of middle school. As I reflect on this time of life, I would describe Brad as quiet and steady. Brad held presence without needing the room's attention; he was welcoming and not abrasive, funny and respectful, and memorable and mysterious.

Shortly after the end of middle school, my family relocated to a town approximately 30 minutes away. This was the time before cell phones, Wi-Fi, social media, or even home computers, resulting in lost connections with many people from my childhood and young adolescence. When smartphones, Wi-Fi, and social media became prevalent in our lives, we reconnected with friends and acquaintances from the past. During this time, connecting via social media was exciting and fun, not littered with divisive politics or social judgments.

Social media reconnected Brad and me and helped close the time gap a bit. Through social media interactions, I was invited to witness the joys of Brad getting married, buying a home, pursuing higher education, and expanding their lives with fur-babies. Sadly, I also became aware of his struggles with substances, history of trauma, and the hardships in his life.

Ironically, although I would call Brad a friend, I couldn't have told you about the hardships he endured as a child and young man. Brad held himself with confidence, a quiet steadiness, a welcoming smile, all while facing devastating hardship outside the walls of school. In the egocentric years of adolescence, I was completely unaware of the events happening in Brad's life that were shaping him and how they would intersect with our lives together.

As you will read in this heartfelt book of strength and vulnerability, Brad endured and persevered; he shares it in hopes of bringing readers on their own journey of acceptance and self-healing. Brad paints a picture with words and opens his heart to the hard-learned lessons of both himself and his wife, Bonnie. Brad found a partner in healing in his wife; together, they love and support each other through trauma, imperfection, and acceptance. It is an honor to invite you to join them on this powerful journey as well.

— **Shelly Ketelhut**

Acknowledgments

Writing *No One Is Normal* has been one of the most challenging and rewarding experiences of my life. This book exists because of the people who stood beside me, believed in me, and reminded me that even in the most challenging times, we never walk alone.

To my wife, Bonnie — thank you for your love, patience, and unshakable belief in me. You are the heart that beats behind every page.

To my mom and stepdad — your love, guidance, and encouragement have carried me farther than words can express. Thank you for teaching me what strength and resilience truly look like.

To my family and friends — your kindness, laughter, and honesty helped keep me grounded while writing these stories. Every late-night talk, message, or word of encouragement mattered more than you'll ever know.

A special thank-you to Shelly — whose thoughtful feedback, careful reading, and beautifully written foreword brought clarity and warmth to this project. Your insight helped shape the final version of this book, and I am deeply grateful.

Finally, to every reader who sees a piece of themselves in these pages — thank you for showing up. This book is for you, too.

Reader's Note

This book is based on real experiences, honest reflections, and lessons learned along the way. It isn't meant to prescribe anyone's life or replace professional advice. Its goal is to offer perspective, encouragement, and a little tough love when it's most needed. Some chapters address complex or sensitive topics. If any part feels overwhelming or triggering, please prioritize your well-being. Take a pause, step back, or discuss it with someone you trust. Above all, remember we're not doctors, lawyers, or therapists. What you'll find here isn't professional advice but stories, ideas, and tools that have helped us (and others) manage challenges. Take what resonates, leave what doesn't, and always seek the support you need for your health, safety, and peace of mind. Throughout this book, you'll find a few readers' notes, meant to inform or advise caution, as the material ahead may cause emotional distress for those who have experienced trauma.

Introduction

When people read about the challenges I've faced or the stories I share in this book, they sometimes assume my entire life has been chaotic. The truth is, it hasn't. Like most people, my life has been a mix of good, bad, and everything in between. There have been moments of laughter, friendship, and purpose that shaped me just as much as the painful ones.

Growing up, I wasn't always lost or struggling. In school, I played sports, wrote poetry, and spent time with friends. I learned the value of teamwork and discipline through experiences like Boy Scouts, which gave me my first sense of structure and belonging. Two things that would later become essential for finding stability in life.

My mother worked very hard and did everything she could to raise me right, and looking back, she did a remarkable job. My stepdad also had a profound influence on me, showing that real strength isn't about toughness; it's about consistency, integrity, and doing the right thing even when no one is watching.

This book is not a traditional memoir or a self-help manual. It's a reflection of what it means to be human: flawed, healing, and still standing. It moves between two perspectives. Some chapters come from my journey and lessons learned through struggle, loss, and rebuilding. Others share Bonnie's story, which deserves to be heard from start to finish. The abuse she endured was only part of the daily reality she lived through, but it offers powerful glimpses into what survival and strength genuinely look like. Her honesty reminds us that healing doesn't come from hiding but from truth.

Bonnie's path hasn't been easy, but it's filled with grace and redemption. One of the most powerful moments in her journey was reuniting with her mother after years of estrangement. That reunion was more than a family moment, and it was a testament to forgiveness, patience, and love finding its way back through the cracks. Her courage to tell her story beside mine gives this book its balance and heart.

Each chapter in this book is meant to stand on its own. Some stories include timelines or dates where context matters, while others explore moments or lessons that don't need a specific time to have meaning. Bonnie's story follows a more chronological path, while mine often moves between reflection and experience. This format allows each story to breathe naturally, connected by theme rather than bound by time.

From the time we're children, we're taught to chase something called *normal.* Normal grades. Normal families. Normal lives. It becomes a quiet standard that few of us ever question. But as we grow older, we realize that *normal* is just a story we've been told. A myth that convinces us to hide the parts of ourselves that don't fit neatly into it.

For a long time, I tried to blend in to survive. At school and work, that meant staying quiet when I wanted to speak. At home, it meant pretending I was fine when I wasn't. Maybe you've done that too, smoothed out your edges to fit into spaces that weren't made for you. The trouble is, the more we pretend, the more disconnected we become from who we truly are.

This book is for anyone who has ever felt out of place. For anyone who has wondered if they're too much or not enough. It's for those who carry silent battles behind a strong face, and for those who have been told to toughen up when what they needed most was to be acknowledged.

The stories you'll read here aren't polished theories or perfect resolutions. They're real experiences — messy, sometimes painful, but always honest. Some may feel familiar. Some may challenge you. That's the point. Healing isn't linear, and there's no single formula for it.

At the end of each chapter, you'll find two short sections: a **Reflection** and a **Reader's Reflection.** The *Reflection* offers a brief insight into the chapter's more profound meaning. A summary of what life taught me through the story you just read. The *Reader's Reflection* is for you. It's not about finding the correct answers but taking a quiet moment to connect your own life to what you've read. These questions are gentle prompts meant to spark thought, honesty, and personal truth. If they are too painful to answer, then feel free to skip. There's no rush. Read at your own pace. Journal if something stirs emotion or curiosity. Pause when it feels heavy. Healing and understanding rarely happen all at once. They may need to happen one reflection at a time.

If you take anything from these pages, let it be this: *You are not broken*. You never were. There is no such thing as normal. There is only you — growing, learning, and changing. And that is more than enough.

REFLECTION:

When I first started writing this book, I didn't know what it would become. I just knew I needed to make sense of everything I'd been through. Maybe it would help someone else do the same. I spent years chasing what I thought was normal, trying to fit into boxes that were never meant for me. It took time to realize that normal was never the goal; being real was. The truth is, we all have moments we hide and stories we carry that shaped us in ways no one else could understand. The stories that follow are pieces of that reminder, one honest chapter at a time.

READER'S REFLECTION:

1. What does "normal" mean to you right now, before reading this book?
2. Where in your life have you felt pressure to appear fine when you weren't?
3. When have you hidden a part of yourself just to fit in? Did it cost you anything?
4. What would it feel like to finally stop chasing normal and start accepting who you really are?
5. How open are you to seeing your story differently by the time you finish these pages?

I

No One Is Normal

My Family Life Explained

I cannot recall how many times I heard the phrases "You are not normal," "That is not how a normal person would do it," or "Why can't you just be normal?" while I was growing up. I had a pretty rough start in my early childhood. My mom and dad were high school sweethearts, and they were happy when they first met. Unfortunately, I joined the party early in the relationship. My mom had me just before her eighteenth birthday, when she was a high school senior.

For my mom, it was about getting out on her own and finally having her own space. She was one of seven children (eight, if you include a brother who passed just after birth) who grew up in poverty in cramped living conditions and had just enough food on the table not to have seconds if you didn't eat fast enough. For my dad, there was partying, drugs, and gambling in his blood, and he wasn't going to deny his right to do those things. He had four siblings who all grew up without a father. His own father left his mother when she became pregnant while he was overseas. Abandonment and instability ran in his family.

My mom and dad tried to make it work, but he couldn't get out of the self-destructive lifestyle that consumed him. They divorced before I had any memories of my father. He then started dating a woman with severe mental health struggles. We called her Sybil. *Fun fact: The name Sybil originates from Greek mythology, where the Sibyls were prophets who spoke with various voices, uttering predictions in an ecstatic frenzy.* That was a fitting nickname.

She always disliked my mom because she had it in her head that my mom and dad were having an affair. She harassed and stalked my mom, and it got so bad that coworkers walked her to the car. My mom would see her parked outside of places, and she would always show up everywhere. I can't imagine being stalked and harassed to that extent, feeling so afraid, uncertain of when or if they're nearby. My mom relocated us halfway across the state, away from all our family. I am sure I would have done the same thing to get away from the situation. Uprooting was a pretty traumatizing event for me, as I was 4 or 5 at the time, and they were all I knew. It was exactly like how every movie portrayed a family moving. It was my mom and I driving away, and the people in the mirror getting smaller and smaller. Eventually, they were gone.

From that point on, we moved around. A lot. It was mainly within the same city, but almost every year, a new school and address would be involved. I would try to fit in and make friends, but they wouldn't last because we had to move again, and I would start at a new school. Part of the reason we moved around a lot later in my childhood was to get away from my mom's abusive ex-husband (not my biological father or current stepdad). I tend to reference him based on the stereotype of the "drunken Irishman." The embodiment of the violent and mean alcoholic. He used to drink, and by drink, I mean absolutely beat his liver into submission. He could polish off close to a case of beer in a night. He had a routine: he would get up, work out, work, and drink.

I cannot remember him talking much at all. He would do these weird Ultimate Warrior-type growls and grunts (from the WWF, now WWE) and do this bizarre neck flex thing with the front of his neck, and it looked like an upside-down folding fan all splayed out. I have blocked him from my mind so profoundly that I can no longer remember any of our conversations. The more I think back, the less I understand what my mom saw in him. For a long time, I believed she stayed because she was afraid of being alone, but as I got older, I began to see it differently. Her fear was rooted in something much more profound. He could be cruel, and when he drank, that cruelty grew darker. She was afraid to leave because she had seen what he was capable of. I saw that side of him, too. Sometimes I got his wrath as well.

My mom and I moved while he was at work. We were temporarily free, but he kept trying to find us. They were both correctional officers, so he found out everything about her, including her new addresses. That is also why we moved around a lot. He would leave cheesecakes, cards, and flowers at our doorstep. I couldn't eat it as we weren't sure if he had poisoned it or anything. Being poor and not having much, this was a bit like torture.

He ended up dating my stepdad's ex-wife. My mom's ex-husband and my stepdad's ex-wife ended up dating. That doesn't just happen. I am sure he stalked my mom, found out they were together, and tried to get back at her. He recently lost his battle with alcohol and died from liver failure. I felt bad for him and his struggle, as I know all too well the fight and strength it takes to get away from alcohol. As a person, he was not a good guy, nor someone I would ever mourn, and that is perfectly normal.

In my first year of high school, I found out that my mom and I were going to move to the country with her boyfriend. That was one hell of a transition going from a city kid to doing farm chores. The transition was miserable, but it taught me the value of work and that your day doesn't end until you complete the tasks at hand. I think that instilled in me a work ethic that I am genuinely grateful for. I went from smoking pot, drinking, and doing acid before I even had a driver's license, to being a transplant farmer. My first summer there was tough: no car, no friends, just farm work, and a man I had only met a dozen times before we moved there. They dated for a while, but my mom didn't let me meet him until later in their relationship. Not sure if it was to protect me or hide me from him so I wouldn't drive him away. My mom married him, and although he's my stepdad, I call him dad. I wouldn't be half the man I am today without him, and I am thankful he's in my life.

The person who hasn't been in my life, my biological father, never grew out of drugs, alcohol, and gambling. I still remember the few times he was going to pick me up so I could spend the summer with him in seventh and eighth grade. The first time, he was going to get me, but he called to say he couldn't, citing car trouble. The second time, he was late, and I was getting antsy, so I took my suitcase and sat on the porch waiting for him to come. He never showed because apparently, he was "arrested" on his way to pick me up. I am not sure if he was or not. My dad was no stranger to jail. When I was very young, he went to prison for selling drugs, and some years later, he went to jail for intent to deliver and possession of a firearm by a convicted felon. He received eight years in prison. I visited him a couple of times and put in more effort to see him than he ever did for me. I was thrilled that he told me he would be there for our wedding, but in the back of my mind, I worried that something would happen, and he wouldn't show up. My father would go on to die from drugs and alcohol two months before Bonnie and I were to be married. He ended up dying from drinking, doing Xanax, and smoking Suboxone. Apparently, people take the medication from the patches and smoke it somehow.

He had moved into my half-brother's apartment. They were huge hard-drug users. They were the ones who gave my dad Suboxone. He told them that he felt sick, and he started puking. He wanted to go to the ER, but they put him to bed, and he never woke up. They didn't want to interrupt their night of doing drugs and risk getting caught. Apparently, Xanax and Suboxone do not mix, and he had a reaction from doing both and died. Usually, when someone like a parent passes in their life, it is devastating, but I felt nothing. I was numb and never felt like this man was my father. One last thing, he didn't show up for.

Why am I telling these things to strangers? Every time I talk to someone about the past, I tell stories. The response I often hear is, "At least you turned out normal." I am sorry, but even if you are Joe Bauers from *Idiocracy* and represent the center of the bell curve and entirely normal, you are still not normal. No one is Normal. No one is, because what is the measuring point of normality? When you look at the big picture and everything that encompasses a human life, there are hundreds of bell curves for every possible measurable scenario. We are compared on everything, from biological traits and personality to health and mental conditions, financial stability, and so forth. While we may be normal on one spectrum, we may not be on another, and so on.

Everything my mom and I went through — the chaos, the instability, and the fear — shaped how I learned to adapt. It taught me that strength does not always come from safety or certainty. Sometimes it comes from simply enduring what you should never have had to face. My childhood was not normal by any standard, but that may be the point. It gave me a front-row seat to see how fragile people can be and how love, even in its smallest moments, can still exist amid the mess. I did not come from a perfect home, but I came from a mother who did the best she could with what she had. Maybe that is all any of us can do.

REFLECTION:

Growing up in chaos taught me that normal was never something to chase. It was a word people used when they wanted others to fit their idea of comfort. My parents were young and still learning who they were, and the instability around me left its mark. For years, I believed that being different meant being wrong, but I see it differently now. What I lived through didn't break me. It shaped me. It gave me the understanding that there is no single version of normal, only the story each person carries and what they choose to make of it.

READER'S REFLECTION:

1. What messages about love, worth, or being normal did you absorb from your family growing up?
2. Which parts of your story were shaped by survival more than choice?
3. How have you learned to separate your parents' struggles from your own identity?
4. What moments from your childhood still echo in how you see yourself today?
5. If forgiveness feels complicated, what would simple acceptance look like instead?

Life on the Farm

Growing up on a farm was not glamorous, but it built character. It also built a strong back and gave me a reputation for fixing almost anything to get back up and running. Downtime on a farm could be devastating as the weather changed every time you looked to the sky. Days started before sunrise, long before most people had rubbed the sleep from their eyes. While others were hitting snooze, I was putting on barn boots and heading to the barn, guided by the sound of the milking machines and the low bellow of impatient cows waiting for their breakfast. The cows did not care whether it was below zero or over 100 degrees. They still needed to be fed, milked, and cared for. The work seemed never-ending. Feeding calves, scraping walkways, sweeping feed, cleaning the barn, and milking cows filled most mornings and evenings, seven days a week.

There were days when the frost bit through my gloves, and the air burned my lungs and exposed skin so sharply that I wondered why anyone would choose this life. Then the sun would rise over the fields, and the smell of hay would mingle with the cold air. For a few quiet moments, the world felt still, and I understood why people stayed.

I learned to drive long before I had a license. My first lessons were not behind the wheel of a car but behind the wheel of a tractor. I learned to back wagons straight, hook up equipment, and work field after field. Those lessons taught me patience and precision long before I ever sat in a classroom.

Each season had its own rhythm. Spring was my favorite. It was the time when everything came back to life after the cold, harsh winter. On the farm, it also meant the season of thawing manure. Cleaning calf pen and bull pens happened almost daily, but sometimes the freeze of the winter air made that a challenge. In the spring, we would have an extra job of cleaning up the thawed waste that tested anyone's stomach. The mix of excrement, urine, and hay that had fermented over the winter stung the nostrils like nothing else. It was the kind of smell that could make even the toughest person gag. Once the land dried, we tilled, fertilized, planted, and sprayed, hoping that Mother Nature would be kind to us.

Summer brought long days and hotter air. The humidity wrapped around you like a wet towel, and the hay fields seemed to stretch forever. We unloaded wagon after wagon, sweat dripping into our eyes and shirts glued to our backs. Some days it was so hot that you could have fried an egg on the concrete, although we never had time to test the theory. The hay always seemed to be ready on the hottest days of the year. Whenever the forecast called for hot and dry weather, I already knew what I would be doing. We also cut wood for the winter. We used to joke that firewood heated you twice: once when you cut it and once when you burned it.

Fall was harvesting time. The air grew crisp, and the fields turned gold. This was when we learned what kind of year it had been. A dry spell, too much rain, a late spring frost, or an early fall could change everything. Farming was not like punching a time clock. What you made at harvest determined the kind of year you would have. Some years were good, but others were hard. There were years when neighbors chose to quit farming because the income didn't cover the expenses. We were fortunate never to face that, but the fear was always at the back of our minds. Back-to-back bad years could hurt or even ruin the most tenured farmer.

Winter gave us a break from the fields, but it came with its own challenges. The Midwest cold tested everyone's patience. When the temperature dropped, everything seemed to go wrong. The silo unloader would jam due to frozen silage. The cows' water drinking cups would freeze, and pipes would burst. Outdoor bulk water tanks iced over, and barn doors froze shut. You learned to fix things fast or freeze while trying. Those long winters made you almost miss the sweat and sunburn of hay season.

There were moments on the farm that you could never forget. I once watched a vet perform surgery on a cow's twisted stomach and install a plastic port in its side. It was fascinating and disgusting at the same time. You do not forget seeing the inside of a cow's stomach up close. When the cows got out, it was chaos. We chased them down roads, into neighbors' yards, or across fields, waving our arms and yelling like we were herding cats. Some followed, some didn't, and others just stood there staring like they were in charge. One day, while I was scraping manure off the walkway, a cow decided to poop and sneeze at the same time. My arm and shoulder were instantly covered. My mom and stepdad laughed so hard that they could barely breathe, and I had to laugh too, once the shock wore off. After that, I learned a valuable lesson: never stand behind the business end of a cow.

When we finally sold the cows, it felt like the end of an era. There were no more 5 a.m. mornings and no more long nights in the barn. I know my parents, who spent more time working on the farm than I did, probably felt relief at not having the everyday-of-the-week grind without a day off. I thought I would feel relief, but what I really felt was a sense of loss. The barn was torn down shortly after. We still worked the land and planted crops, but the heart of the farm was gone. The dairy had given us a purpose and a rhythm that tied us together.

Farming taught me more about life than any classroom ever could. It taught me resilience, patience, and pride in a job well done. It also taught me that success is not measured by comfort. It is measured by the dirt under your nails, the sweat on your brow, and the honesty in your work.

REFLECTION:

Looking back, I realize the farm gave me everything I needed to understand life. It taught me to work hard even when no one was watching, to stay grounded when things got tough, and to find humor in the mess. It showed me that hard work didn't just build muscle; it also built character. The long days weren't just about getting the job done. They were about learning discipline, patience, and pride in doing things the right way. When my parents sold the cows and tore down the barn, the landscape changed, but the lessons stayed.

The rhythm of farm life shaped who I became, and even now, I carry those lessons into everything I do.

READER'S REFLECTION:

1. What memories of simplicity or hard work have stayed with you the longest, and how has that helped you in certain situations?
2. When was the last time you felt truly grounded in something ordinary?
3. Has a significant change happened in your life, where you miss something from it?
4. Who in your life modeled quiet strength or consistency that shaped your values?
5. What do you miss most about the times when life felt slower, quieter, or more intentional?

Coming Full Circle

I don't remember meeting my grandfather on my dad's side, but my mom told me that he met me when I was a baby. For years, I was afraid to reach out to him because I didn't want to be rejected. Rejection had already carved enough scars into my life, and I did not think I could handle one more. I was told he had moved on, built a new life, and did not want any of the past family drama. My grandma tried to get him to claim other kids she said were his, but the timing didn't add up since he was overseas. I grew up believing he did not want anything to do with me. I carried that feeling for years, and it kept me from trying.

In my early thirties, I worked up the courage to call him. I did not know what to expect, but when he answered, his voice was kind and familiar in a way that caught me off guard. He was genuinely happy to hear from me. That moment changed everything. I finally flew down to Tennessee to meet him, his wife, my uncle, his wife, their twin daughters, and their son. It felt surreal, like stepping into a missing piece of my life. Each visit after that built a bond that felt like it had been missing for decades. When I graduated with my master's degree, they all came up north to see me walk across that stage. Seeing them in the crowd meant more than they will ever know. My grandpa was the reason I became a Freemason. He was a 32nd-degree Scottish Rite Mason, and through that, I came to understand a deeper kind of brotherhood and legacy.

Bonnie and I had been together for a while when she finally got the opportunity to reconnect with her own family, who lived only about an hour away down in Tennessee. Life has a strange way of weaving stories together.

We began visiting her family whenever we went south as well, and she got to meet relatives she had not seen since she was a child. Those visits were full of laughter, awkward introductions, and quiet healing. We both found something we did not realize we had lost. Family.

In September 2022, my grandpa's wife, my step-grandma, passed away. Bonnie and I flew down for the funeral, and seeing him broke my heart. He had fallen, hurt his back and foot, and could barely walk and was mostly bound to a wheelchair. He looked tired, both from grief and age. I was worried he would not make it through the holidays. We promised to come back for Thanksgiving so he wouldn't be alone, and we did. Spending that week with him helped all of us. He smiled more, talked more, and for the first time in a while, he seemed lighter.

When we went back in May 2023, he was like a new man. He moved more easily, laughed more, and had his spark back. A large group of us went to the World Championship Barbecue Cooking Contest, one of the best BBQ events in the country. The smell alone was enough to make you hungry even after a big meal. The smoke, music, and crowd were something special. If you ever get the chance to go, you should. Be sure you know someone on the inside, because that is where the real magic and food happen. That day felt good. It was one of those rare moments where life paused long enough to let you feel grateful.

A few months later, my grandfather met a new woman. She was of Filipino descent, thin, tiny, 15 years younger, and was also widowed. She seemed quiet and polite — maybe distant — and kind enough. There was a significant language barrier as she spoke very broken English, but he seemed really happy. She had the picture-perfect resting bitch face look to her. They dated for a few months and decided to move in together. Neither one wanted to go to the other's house because of memories, so they sold their homes in Tennessee and moved to Mississippi, near the ocean. Once they moved in together, things changed. Communication with him became rare. His son and I barely heard from him. Bonnie and I had a trip planned to see them. Before the trip, he mentioned he was really sick and said we shouldn't come down, just three days before we were to travel. We told him we were coming anyway, as we had already booked the trip and didn't care if he was sick.

When we flew down to visit, he looked and sounded fine, but looked a little rundown. Their house was cluttered from floor to ceiling with trinkets and knick-knacks. Both cars were parked in the driveway because there was no room in the garage due to all her antiques. We were the first of his family to see inside the home. No space felt like him. He sat on the couch, looked stressed, and appeared to be under duress. We only saw him for ten minutes out of the five-day trip. He mentioned going out for food later, and he said no when we asked to join. We offered to go to church with him, and he said no again. It hurt more than I expected. We had spent thousands of dollars to visit, and it felt like he was already slipping away. She wasn't sick and never even came out to see us. Sadly, I said things out of hurt and frustration during that trip, and I later regretted it. On his eighty-fourth birthday, I called and apologized. He never apologized back, and that did not matter. I was not looking for one. I just wanted peace between us before time ran out.

After that trip, his calls were short and strained. He usually didn't answer, and when he did call back, it seemed to be only when she was not around. The moment she came near, the conversation would end with a quick "I've got to go." His son told me he barely heard from him, even though they were very close. He hasn't even been invited to their new place. People close to the situation said she was controlling and mean, and maybe that was the life he had grown used to. His late wife had been the same way. Perhaps he did not know how to live without someone else in control.

In the spring of 2025, my uncle, his wife, and their kids came up to visit. We spent time catching up, seeing the sights, and even got them to tour a rival football team's stadium. He was impressed, and even admitted it out loud. It was great having them here; unfortunately, we all wished Grandpa had come too. The previous version of him, before his new relationship, would have come. We had some great conversations and plenty of laughs. One story from my aunt surprised and shocked all of us. She told us about a time when a man was flirting with her at Walmart, complimenting her outfit and shoes. He mentioned how nice her hands looked, then said he liked her toenail paint and asked to see it up close because his eyesight was poor. She obliged, and the next thing she knew, the guy leaned down, pulled off her shoe, and put her foot in his mouth. Right there in Walmart, this guy was sucking her toes. We all burst out laughing so hard we cried. It was one of those stories that you could not make up even if you tried.

After the humor faded, the reality of life kicked back in. The conversation shifted to the twins, who were getting ready to head off to college — one staying close to home and the other moving away. Their younger brother had just gotten his driver's license and was starting to find his way in life. You hear people say it as you get older: "Where does the time go?" Standing there that night, it finally made sense. They flew back home, and the present became the past.

Now my talks with Grandpa are shorter. He sounds tired, distracted, and distant. I put forth the effort to still call and check in. Sometimes I get a glimpse of the old him: a small laugh, a story about events going on near him, or a joke that reminds me who he really is. That is enough for me now. I have learned that you cannot control how people live or who they choose to love. You can only decide how you show up.

Finding my dad's long-lost side of the family gave me something I did not know I needed: a sense of belonging. It showed me that even when the past is broken, the future can still be built. My dad never got that chance, but I did. That is what coming full circle really means: finding peace in the space between what was lost and what was found.

REFLECTION:

Family has a way of surprising you. Sometimes, it brings laughter that fills the room, and other times, silence that leaves you searching for words. Reconnecting with my grandpa, uncle, and their family reminded me how quickly time moves and how easily it can slip away. One moment, you are sharing stories and laughing until your sides hurt, and the next, everyone is older, busier, and scattered across different places. The visits, the meals, and even the strange stories in between are what hold us together. It is easy to take those moments for granted until they are gone. Coming full circle reminded me that family is not about how often you see each other, but how deeply you stay connected. It is about showing up, even when the conversations are short, and finding peace in the love that remains.

READER'S REFLECTION:

1. Who in your life do you wish you could reconnect with, and what would you say if you had the chance?
2. How has time changed the way you see your family or your past relationships?
3. What fears or assumptions have kept you from reaching out to someone who once mattered?
4. When have you found healing in forgiveness, even if it didn't come with closure?
5. What does "coming full circle" mean to you, and where might that moment still be waiting in your own story?

What is the Definition of Normal?

L et's start with the easy part. Let's define what normal is. This should be quick and easy. Right? According to Merriam-Webster, the definition for normal is as follows:

Reader's Note: You may skip the detailed definition if preferred, as it is included for reference to provide context.

Normal – Adjective

1. a: conforming to a type, standard, or regular pattern: characterized by that which is considered usual, typical, or routine.
   b: according with, constituting, or not deviating from a norm, rule, procedure, or principle.
2. occurring naturally.
3. a: approximating the statistical average or norm.
   b: generally free from physical or mental impairment or dysfunction: exhibiting or
   marked by healthy or sound functioning.
   c: not exhibiting defect or irregularity.
   d: within a range considered safe, healthy, or optimal.
4. a: of a solution
   having a concentration of one gram equivalent of solute per liter.
   b: containing neither basic hydroxyl nor acid hydrogen
   normal silver phosphate.

c: not associated.

normal molecules.

d: having a straight-chain structure.

normal butyl alcohol

5. PERPENDICULAR

   especially perpendicular to a tangent (see TANGENT entry 1 sense 3) at a point of tangency.

6. of a subgroup

   having the property that every coset produced by operating on the left by a given element is equal to the coset produced by operating on the right by the same element.

7. relating to, involving, or being a normal curve or normal distribution.

   normal approximation to the binomial distribution.

8. of a matrix

   having the property of commutativity under multiplication by the transpose of the matrix (see MATRIX sense 5a) each of whose elements is a conjugate (see CONJUGATE entry 1 sense 2b) complex number with respect to the corresponding element of the given matrix.

Normal – Noun

1. a form or state regarded as the norm: STANDARD.
2. one that is normal.
3. a: a normal line.

   b: the portion of a normal line to a plane curve between the curve and the x-axis.

Source: Merriam–Webster.com Dictionary, Merriam–Webster, Inc. Retrieved from: https://www.merriam–webster.com/dictionary/normal

Fun fact: the word normal comes from the Latin normâlis, meaning a right angle (90 degrees), and it is also referred to as a carpenter's square.

Let's begin with the idea of conforming. When you try to be normal, you are essentially conforming to a type, standard, or regular pattern. Human beings are as unique as snowflakes. Don't believe it? Look at your fingerprints, retina scans, or dental records as each identifies you. Go deeper still, and your DNA is the blueprint that makes you who you are.

Our entire lives, we are told to conform to society's expectations, even though none of us technically do. Years of conditioning groom us to fit in to be what we are expected to be. We are easier to control when we follow the patterns. When we don't, we are labeled as abnormal. I didn't create the rules of government, but that's how they work. Someone broke a rule, so a new one was written to penalize the infraction.

As a kid, I also tested boundaries, seeing what I could get away with. Sometimes I slipped by, sometimes I got caught. Nothing terrible, just harmless rebellion. In middle school, a craze started: tight-rolling the bottoms of your pants. Something so simple carried real pressure to conform. I refused. I didn't like the fad, and I felt like a pariah. People stared and whispered like I was a diseased leper. Some even offered to help by rolling my pants for me. One student told me that people were talking about me because I hadn't done it. As the new kid, I already felt like the outsider, so what was the point? I wasn't going to pretend just to fit in. I'm sure you've felt social pressure like that, too.

It's not just school-age fads. This continues into adulthood. Drinking is a good example: alcoholism carries stigma, but drinking itself is considered normal. That divide creates judgment. If you drink around non-drinkers, you risk being labeled an alcoholic. If you don't drink around drinkers, you're judged for abstaining. Smoking works the same way. Neither is as innocent as a fashion fad, although both show how society pressures us to conform or risk judgment.

Some define normal as occurring naturally. I disagree. Everything in nature is natural, even disasters. That doesn't mean everything is normal. If life always went exactly as expected, it would be pretty uninteresting. We remember what is unusual: surprises, disruptions, and memorable stories. Think back. Can you remember an ordinary Tuesday six months ago? Probably not. But you can recall a day when something unusual happened.

I have plenty of memories, good and bad. One stands out because it wasn't routine. I often bought four concert tickets, hoping friends would come. Usually, they couldn't afford them or didn't like the band, so I gave extras away. One time, I booked a downtown hotel to make a day of it and enjoy the big city experience.

When we pulled up to the hotel, my friend suddenly asked, "What did you do?" I thought I had cut someone off. Then we saw them, bus after bus unloading little people for a convention at our hotel. Inside, the lobby was packed, and aside from the staff, my friend and I were the tallest people there. While waiting in line, the hostess waved me forward to the desk. Then I felt a tug on my pant leg. A little person said, "Excuse me, you cut in front of me. I was next." Without thinking, I blurted, "I'm sorry, I didn't see you there."

The lobby went so silent that I could hear my own heartbeat. My words would have been harmless in most situations, but not this one. We ended up booking a hotel hosting a national convention of little people, which was a big deal for their community. That moment burned into my memory because it was so unusual. I grew up watching *Little People, Big World*, a show about a family that faced challenges together and made the most of their lives. To outsiders, their life wasn't normal; to them, it was. Seeing hundreds of little people at the convention wasn't normal for me, but it was for them. That's perception. If ninety-eight percent of your town were little people, the definition of *normal* would flip.

Another part of the definition is the absence of defects or abnormalities, or conformity to an established norm. Averages only tell part of the story. In terms of height, weight, eye color, blood type, or personality, most of us are average in some ways and outliers in others. Having ADHD, depression, albinism, dwarfism, or baldness places you outside the mean. Being outside the mean does not make you less. It makes you who you are. Those traits can bring both challenges and strengths. The key is learning to adapt and work with what makes you different.

It took me years to understand that you never really know what someone is going through because you're not living in their head. Like a duck on a pond, calm above the surface, paddling hard beneath, people may appear fine while silently struggling. I know this well as I'm very self-aware, and also my harshest critic. Others can be hard on me; I'm harder on myself. Perfectionism can push you or break you. Is it OCD? Past trauma? Both? Our genetics are the foundation, and the environment builds the house. Sometimes, even perception helps remodel it. That's why a good suburban kid might spiral, or why some people repeat cycles of bad relationships, financial struggles, or emotional pain. The point is this: no one is truly normal. We all carry issues, quirks, and struggles. We are not alone in this feeling.

REFLECTION:

Growing up, I spent a lot of time chasing what other people called "normal." I thought it was a goal or something I could earn if I just acted the right way or blended in enough. Over time, I learned that normal isn't real. It shifts depending on who you ask and where you are in life. The harder I tried to reach it, the more disconnected I became from who I really was. Once I stopped trying to fit into someone else's version of normal, I finally started to find peace in my own.

READER'S REFLECTION:

1. Who taught you what "normal" was supposed to look like, and do you still believe it?
2. When have you caught yourself comparing your life to someone else's definition of success or happiness?
3. What parts of yourself have you hidden to fit into someone else's version of "normal"?
4. How would your life feel different if you stopped measuring yourself against others?
5. What if "normal" was never the goal, just being real was?

We Are Not Normal, Now What?

When you zoom all the way out (well, as far as humans are concerned), we are Homo sapiens, classified by taxonomy like all living things. We are the top of the food chain, except when we aren't. You know the videos or images you see when there is a fat boa with a lump of digested person inside of it, or a gator taking a swim on the surface of the water with a dead human in its mouth. Sorry to put that image in your head. Sadly, we think nothing like that could happen to us; however, we are sometimes food for other species in their fight for survival.

Our opposable thumbs have given us the ability to use tools or weapons to help mitigate those risks. Those tools have given us the ability to create elaborate structures to stave off predators, withstand extreme weather, keep out intruders, or resist Jehovah's Witnesses (am I right?). We also developed capabilities to store food for extended periods without it being stolen by poachers or rotting.

Human beings were originally nomads. While we are still somewhat nomadic today, transportation has enabled us to travel anywhere, visit, and return home in hours rather than weeks or months. Thank goodness, I couldn't imagine having to stay somewhere you have traveled to for long periods, or vice versa. Unless it was on a beach in the tropics, chances are it would end up being at that weird uncle's place, where you are sure someone is chained in the basement. Our early ancestors had to travel to where the food was available. Your local grocer now carries a variety of regional and exotic cuisines you never could have imagined, let alone out of season, unless they were preserved or fermented. You can travel the globe with the click of a mouse. Everything has gotten super convenient. Everything has improved significantly for us humans, except for one thing: our purpose.

That is one thing most of us humans struggle with. I know when I was younger, I had a lot of angst. Growing up poor with a single mother, I didn't have much to look forward to. As I entered my teens and twenties, it intensified further. It is fantastic looking back at how, even though I had things pretty good, I still struggled because I felt I didn't have a purpose. Don't get me wrong, I still struggle with it and say, "Why bother," but not as often. Our purpose can be anything that drives the life you lead and how you want it to be. It can be existential to continue providing stepping-stones for evolution by procreating.

Your purpose can be societal, religious, political, career-driven, or even rooted in hobbies. Whether that feels unfortunate or fortunate depends on your perspective on how society is structured. Ultimately, what you do in life is your choice. You have the freedom to do whatever you want. For example, when I say fortunate, in my travels to India, they are a caste system passed down through families. You may be limited in what you can do, depending on your family's status. We have that to some extent here, although in India, it is a stringent social hierarchy that even includes arranged marriages. The only way to move to a higher caste is to obey the rules in the one you are born into and hope for change in the next life. So, you are stuck, and there is no way around it. We have that to an extent here, only not to the extent that you would have to die and be reborn to change.

When I traveled to India, the people were terrific, and the food was equally so. It was such a beautiful and vibrant culture. The living conditions were poor at best for lower-caste members. The wealthy lived in flats, much like most people in larger cities. There were all too many people sleeping on the streets; most of those people lived in sub-poverty conditions or the slums of India. If you get bored, you can explore Google Earth in Mumbai, zoom in, and look around the Dharavi Slums. For example, you will see some of the large, semi-hut-style living conditions all tied together. I spent most of my time in Mumbai and Pune in India. I didn't get to travel to many rural places when I was there. Still, the cities were hot, humid, dusty, and smoky from the two-stroke engines of motorcycles and rickshaws. It made breathing difficult, much like the US metropolises affected by leaded gas and smog of old. Having experienced that, when people complain to me about the living conditions here or how dirty a city is, they really have no idea how amazing we have it here.

In the US, you have more opportunities; in comparison, our education system does not help people understand what life is about and what is truly needed. We learn about the history of our nation, but we do not teach current events to help shape the future. Children need to be taught both sides of a story and to extrapolate data to reach their own conclusions. There is no training on the time value of money or on building and maintaining a strong credit score. Some people were lucky enough to take a class in record-keeping or accounting. Do not get me wrong, our education system is excellent and provides a comprehensive learning experience overall. Still, there are areas we could improve to help people better understand life. The more access you have to money and resources, the more opportunities you have to transcend those situations.

Not being normal is what makes us human. We are constantly searching for purpose, meaning, and a sense of belonging in a world that often rewards the surface and overlooks the depth beneath it. We forget that progress was never made by people who fit perfectly into the system; it is by those who questioned it. Each of us can change direction, to learn, to unlearn, and to create something better from what we have been given. Purpose is not something you stumble upon; it is something you grow into through awareness, struggle, and choice. When you understand that not being normal stops feeling like a problem and starts feeling like a privilege, it becomes a source of pride.

REFLECTION:

Recognizing that we are not normal can feel both liberating and terrifying. For a long time, I believed being different meant there was something wrong with me. Letting go of that belief forced me to look at who I really am instead of who I thought I was supposed to be. It made me question what kind of life I want to live and who I want to become. When I stopped trying to meet everyone else's expectations and accepted that I am not like everyone else, I gained the freedom to grow and the courage to live in a way that finally feels true to me.

READER'S REFLECTION:

1. What parts of yourself have you spent the most time trying to change just to belong?
2. When did you first realize that being different might actually be your strength?
3. What would it mean to live without apology for who you are?
4. How has comparison held you back from peace or joy?
5. What small act could you do today that feels true to you, not to anyone else's expectations?

Don't Let the Past Affect the Present

Why am I bringing all this up, and what does it matter? Life is a long road for most, though not so much for the less fortunate. Why make it feel longer by constantly living in the past? I like the thought of the past, just as it is, the past. It was a reference point for something we had done. It is not a destination point for the future. We can always change the direction we are going in the present by adjusting our path. The problem arises when people want to see a change but do not make any course corrections. That is the definition of insanity: doing the same thing over and over again and expecting different results. We cannot dwell on the past or keep repeating the same patterns. I really want to drive this point home because we control our present and future. No one can control what has happened, as it is already a part of the past. We can learn from and use it as a catalyst for change. It took me many years to forgive myself for the things from the past. Not just what I had done, but also what had been done to me. I actually weaponized those things, so when I failed, I wouldn't be disappointed and would have built-in excuses. I was my own worst enemy, self-sabotaging at every phase of my life.

We can be our own worst critics, can't we? For example, I ended up buying a small starter home back in the city. It was amazing how many people had started new lives and moved away, just five years after graduating high school. It left me without really knowing anyone anymore. I did have one friend whom I called often. I started hanging out with him and a group that would always meet at the bar, and this routine continued into my thirties. It was with that group of friends that alcohol was a necessity and was always the common denominator, regardless of who I hung out with in that group.

Once, while bar hopping, we walked to the next bar, cut through a school parking lot, and ended up at a fence. Everyone helped everyone over. I looked back for one of our group members, and he was taking a piss, so I decided to wait, but he was sitting on the phone. I grew impatient, so I jumped the six-foot-tall fence, and when I landed, I felt intense pain when I took my first step. I hobbled to the nearest bar and called a friend to pick me up. I found out I broke my right heel. I ended up on short-term disability for the whole summer due to the injury. I completely depleted my 401(k) with partying and putting gas in my buddy's boat. Talk about a losing investment. Looking back, I should have conducted an honest self-assessment because I completely veered off course.

After that summer, it was work, school, and drinking. At one point, I went to a doctor because I couldn't shut my mind off and couldn't sleep. Alcohol on its own will cause the false feeling of sleep, but it is actually a nightly stupor coma. The doctor prescribed Xanax to me around the beginning of the opioid crisis. I didn't even know what it was, but I knew it helped me sleep like the dead. Fast-forward a year and add a housing market crash. I ended up getting laid off, and without insurance, I could not afford my prescription. I took my last one the night before, woke up the next day, and started feeling off more as the day went by. I still remember to this day how rough a withdrawal was from taking Xanax long-term, as I was taking it for close to two years. I ended up going back to the farm for a few days because I was in an awful spot and didn't know what else to do.

Alcohol itself could not help me quell my withdrawals. Mainly due to taking them when I was drinking, hindsight is always 20/20. It got to the point where I spent three full days researching Xanax and found a way to withdraw safely from it, due to my severe insomnia. It was a drug that addiction clinics said Sorry, we cannot help you, you need to find someone else who can. Trust me, I did call to talk with them as I was desperate. With Xanax having a fast withdrawal rate, typically 12 to 24 hours, withdrawal starts from the drug. I found a way to safely withdraw using a slower-acting opioid to titrate off of it. It was roughly a 6-month process. It is essential to discuss this with your physician if you are taking this and want to wean off, as I am not a doctor. I am only discussing how I was able to stop them comfortably. You can find charts for the conversion rates and medical documents to bring to this discussion. I used charts like the one on benzo.org.uk/bzequiv.htm, which references the work of Professor Heather Ashton of the UK, who produced the Ashton manual. I printed off the manual and brought it to the doctor, who said that there was no way to stop taking the drug. That was not a good enough answer for me. Thank goodness, because the withdrawals I was facing were nasty, and I was only taking a normal three times a day dose of .5 mg.

I have never experienced anything like that and wish never to experience them again. To give you a glimpse of the symptoms that I went through. Everything was loud and bright. Every time I tried to fall asleep, my body would jerk to the point it looked like I was marching, so there was no sleeping. I had to strain to urinate and could barely defecate. I had no appetite. I could not form coherent thoughts. My teeth felt like they were rotating in their sockets. I started to see things that weren't there. The next stage was seizure on the withdrawal cycle, but fortunately, I started the other regimen in time to stop the potential seizures. I really had to convince the doctor to help me titrate off this drug. What amazes me is how many people were stuck on this drug and how many people were in misery like I was while I was doing my research. It makes me sick the number of addictive medications prescribed under the pretense that they are safe for everyday use, but there is nothing set up to get people off the drug if they want to wean off of it.

Despite everything, I continued attending school and began working with a different company. I thought I had hit rock bottom and was on the way back to feeling better. I must have found a trap door and hit a new level. I do not blame anyone for the things that have happened in my life, especially things that I had complete control over. I cannot state that enough. The next series of events was my fault, and things could have been much worse. Trust me, some of the people who have done things very similar to me have ended up hurting or killing someone and gone to jail or prison. So, I didn't have it so bad. It was my wake-up call.

I got into an argument with the person I was dating, so I decided to drive to the bar six blocks away. There was a game that day, so I decided to have a Sunday Funday and drink at the bar. After all, the longest relationship I have ever had was with alcohol, and it rarely let me down. It was always there to comfort me when I needed it. So, many beers and shots later, I decided to get behind the wheel. Instead of leaving my car and walking to get it in the morning, I did the one thing you should never do: I got behind the wheel. I made it two blocks before getting pulled over. I turned in front of a police officer and swerved to overcompensate due to my impairment. I blew a 0.19. I was arrested for OWI. The whole process was costly and embarrassing. I made the mistake, pleaded guilty, and was willing to accept the punishments handed down for my actions.

I was also part of the newer ignition interlock program at the time. That is where they install a breathalyzer in your car, which requires you to blow into the device randomly every 5 to 20 minutes while driving to monitor your blood alcohol level. If you do not pass, your horn will go off, and eventually it will kill your car. There were mornings when I couldn't start my car because I had drunk the night before and had to go back inside to brush my teeth and tongue again to get to work. Talk about embarrassing. It was no one's fault but my own. I chose this path, and as I stated before, at least I never hurt anyone. The punishment worked. I did not drink and drive again, but it also messed with my psyche. I did not want another OWI, so rather than do the smart thing and quit drinking, I stopped being social and started drinking alone at home. I would occasionally take an Uber or taxi, but I mostly stayed inside. I would work, come home, and drink while doing schoolwork as it was online. I became a recluse and continued my relationship with alcohol.

Now I could have just continued on that cycle, but eventually I woke up and really wanted to change my life. I was sick of the daily drinking and drinking to stop the feelings from the night before. Rather than use alcohol to numb my feelings, I actually started to face my demons. I did not go to rehab or to AA, not that there is anything wrong with that route. I ended up using a couple of e-books to listen to while driving. The books were *The Stop Drinking Expert* by Craig Beck and *Alcohol is Shit* by Paul Churchill. I still listen to them from time to time when I feel I need to. I also downloaded Reframe, an app for quitting or reducing drinking. It was another big reason I was able to stop. It gives you daily lessons and journaling to help you understand the reasons behind things. It also has online meetings that you can attend multiple times a day. If you are in a vicious alcohol cycle, please reach out and get help. Some things work better for others, and this worked well for me. What works for one does not work for all. Find something that will work for you.

Through that time, there was a smattering of relationships, but as I stated before, I was in a relationship with alcohol, so I didn't have room for anyone else. Through this journey, I discovered myself and realized that I am worth more than my own brain was willing to admit. I've learned that it's essential to find someone whose ambition and drive align with our own. Some people are content simply existing, and that's perfectly fine, but be honest about what kind of life you want. When two people move through life at different speeds or with varying levels of purpose, it can create frustration and distance. I've seen how that imbalance can slowly chip away at peace and connection. We want to have that same energy in another person more than we often admit. Choosing a partner sometimes feels like choosing a career. We invest most of our time either at work or with the person we love. If neither brings fulfillment, then it becomes challenging to give our best to either.

The past will always be part of who we are, and it should never be the driver of who we become. Every mistake, heartbreak, and poor decision can be a lesson if we allow it to be. We cannot rewrite the past, but we can write what happens next. The moment we stop letting old pain decide how we live today, we start the process of healing. It took me a long time to understand that forgiveness is not about forgetting; it is about releasing the hold that pain has on the present. When we finally learn to do that, life begins to move forward again, and so do we

REFLECTION:

The past has a way of haunting us. I spent a long time letting my past dictate how I saw myself. Every mistake, every loss, and every painful memory became a reason to hold back or doubt my own growth. For years, I thought moving on meant pretending those things never happened, but that only kept them alive in different ways. Healing, for me, has been about facing those memories and taking away their control. My past shaped me, but it doesn't own me anymore. I can't change where I've been, but I can decide the type of person I want to be today.

READER'S REFLECTION:

1. What moments from your past still hold power over how you see yourself today?
2. When you think about forgiveness, is there someone, including yourself, who still needs it?
3. How do old wounds show up in your reactions or relationships now?
4. What would it look like to forgive your past without letting it define you?
5. What slight shift could help you focus more on where you're going instead of where you've been?

Life Is Hard, Don't Make It Harder

L ife can challenge us. DO NOT add opportunities to make it harder. One of the most important things I can pass along to anyone is that the path to success is not a straight line; bad decisions can cause you to start over on your perceived success. When we are younger, we do not associate life with the same risks that we encounter when we get older. Everything we do that puts us in a risky situation increases the odds of something bad happening. Persistence and determination have always been key for me, and sometimes luck played its part, too. The hardest lesson was realizing that I was often the one standing in my own way. I had to learn to stop tripping over my own doubts and excuses before I could move forward. Let me explain.

I mentioned earlier that I moved out to the farm after my first year of high school. Looking back now, it's easy to see what came next. Life took a turn most parents probably expect when a teenager gets uprooted and thrown into a whole new world. After learning about the move, my grades dropped from A's and B's to C's and D's. I was finally feeling like I had some semblance of a foundation after being at the same place for 2.5 years and attending only one new school during that time, transitioning naturally to high school. That was the longest I had been at the same school by a long shot. I had made some friends, and we had to move again. I think I had a 1.9 GPA (D+) after my first year. I had a whole summer to work on the farm and reset. My sophomore year was so-so. Then, in my Junior and Senior years, I really excelled and was in honors classes. I raised my grade point average to 2.74, which I was proud of, given the turnaround from my first year.

I didn't think I would be going to college, so I bypassed the SATs. I did not study, yet I took the ACT. I got a 21. That is good enough to get you into a junior college or college extension. Again, I doubted myself and didn't think I would go to school. I changed my mind and applied to a few schools, but I got rejected. My mom worked at a school and spoke with the Dean about my application, and I still didn't get accepted. I worked in construction for a couple of years before deciding to attend school. I would burn, blister, peel, and repeat. I knew my fair skin wouldn't be able to do this the rest of my life, so I had to do something.

I want to be clear. Making the path more complicated only creates pain. I am sharing my missteps and instructions on what not to do. When I was 20, I started school. I attended a university extension to begin my general education classes. I was able to live on campus at another school, as the extension itself didn't have living quarters. I was excited to go out on my own and live in the dorms. School started fine until I joined a fraternity. Now, there is nothing wrong with joining a fraternity if you enter for the right reasons. I joined one where some members drank heavily. You can guess what my priorities were, and I was a pledge who got "persuaded" to drink and didn't focus on my studies. I got suspended for the semester and dropped out. I received eighteen credits and a shitty fraternity paddle that I never gave to my big brother, because I dropped out of the fraternity as well. I also had to pay back a student loan for the next four years.

After a few more unexciting years of working in mills, I bought a house. During that time, I also started dating someone who was starting school, and I felt it was essential for me to do the same, so I decided to go back to school. I took a placement test at the technical college and scored among the highest they had seen in all categories. Which was a good feeling, as it assured me that I wasn't stupid; it was a matter of lack of effort on my end. Looking back, I think my affiliation with alcohol was what kept lifting the pen on my page of success. If I had 99 problems, 98 of them were due to alcohol.

The devil is in the details throughout this book, particularly in some of those stories. After three years, I earned an associate degree and made the dean's list multiple times. I was accepted into a university and decided to pursue further education. I pursued a degree in Operations Management and graduated with honors. The program manager inquired about my interest in joining the master's program in Operations and Supply Management. I thought about it and really wanted to continue. I would be the second in my family to earn an advanced degree. I thought I was the only one until I met my estranged grandfather.

Expanding my education took nine years; during that time, I attended school and worked over 40 hours a week. One of the things I did was trade the window of having children for that time. I wasn't dating anyone I'd want to have kids with until I met my wife. We both decided that we did not want children. She had a very rough life and was in a horrible relationship with tons of trauma. She was also battling severe blood pressure issues and didn't want to risk losing her.

Looking back, I realize that life will always find ways to test you, but most of the obstacles I faced were ones I built myself. I was the one who let the distractions steer me off course. The difference between the person I was and the person I became was not luck or intelligence. It was learning to stop creating my own storms. Life is already hard enough without adding more weight to carry. When I took responsibility for my choices, focused on growth, and stopped fighting against myself, I finally gave life a chance to get easier. It will still hurt sometimes, but at least I stopped getting in my own way.

REFLECTION:

Life has always come with its own challenges. Pain, loss, and uncertainty are part of being human, but I used to make things more complicated than they needed to be. I held on to habits, people, and patterns that kept me stuck when I should have been learning to let go. It took time to realize that life will test me enough on its own, and I don't need to add more struggle. The more I focus on what I can control and release what I can't, the more peace I find. My strength comes from simplifying what I carry so I have enough energy left to face what truly matters.

READER'S REFLECTION:

1. When life feels heavy, what patterns or habits make it even more complicated than it needs to be?
2. How do you usually respond when things don't go as planned, with patience or pressure?
3. What does giving yourself grace look like in difficult situations?
4. When was the last time you made things easier for yourself by letting go of control?
5. What's a straightforward thing you can start doing today to bring more ease into your life?

Relapsed

At the time of writing this book, I did relapse for a short period. Drinking is a very tough habit to break. Some days go well, and some go off the rails. Staying away from alcohol takes time and effort, and when life gets hard, I really have to focus on not falling back into the addiction loop. Regrettably, I let the boogeyman back into my life. Thankfully, it was only for a few months, but I could really tell the difference between being sober for a long time and drinking every day, in such a short time frame. It amazed me how horrible I felt the longer I drank like that. My body prioritized getting the poison out of my system and neglected the normal functions that needed to happen.

So, what happened? I was doing well on my sober journey and felt great. Unfortunately, I was struggling with my new job. The stress, pressure, and lack of support were starting to take their toll on me. My wife's health was also weighing heavily on me. I felt helpless when there was nothing I could do to fix it. All of it started adding up, and one day I went to the gas station and bought a pint of Kessler. That was the beginning. I never really had hangovers, but I would feel off the next day, so I kept going with the daily drinking cycle. In this book, I talk about the position I left due to multiple issues; this was the timeline. After leaving that job, I was in a dark place, broken, without work, and my wife's health was in decline. I was drinking a 750 ml bottle of booze a day. After two months, I started drinking in the morning and kept going until I passed out. Once that cycle started, it took a lot of effort to get out of it. Escaping this took more effort than falling ever did, as it pulled like gravity while I circled the drain.

When someone is stuck in that cycle and cannot stop on their own, they have to seek help to break free. I had to use whatever tools I could find in the toolbox to escape. For me, it was a slow process of fighting the urge to drink in the morning, cutting back down to a pint at night, and then finally stopping again. A few things helped along the way. I kept my mind busy with classes and online training, and my wife started juicing. Within three months, she was almost back to normal from her debilitating health issues. She became an entirely different person. If someone had seen her four months earlier, they would not believe the difference now. Her health issues were mainly managed, and her medication went from twelve pills down to four. Even though I was not working yet, having her health mostly restored helped me more than I can describe.

Things will always happen in life, and they will not always go as planned. That is okay. I have to make healthy choices about how I manage my emotions. Alcohol use disorder or drug use might feel like the easy way out to numb the pain, but it never solves the problem. On my journey to become alcohol free, I have relapsed a couple of times. Each time, the relapse was shorter before I stopped again. I am not proud of relapsing, but I am proud of the effort I put into pulling myself out of the black hole.

One of the key moments came when my wife told me she was worried about my drinking. She did not yell or argue. She just said it softly and calmly. That helped more than any explosion of anger ever could have. It also helped that I was willing to listen. At that point, I knew that if she was that concerned, I had to change. The last thing I want is for her to watch someone she loves slowly kill himself. I could not live with that on my conscience. She does not deserve that, especially after everything she had endured.

I have to remind myself that people love me and care about me. Sometimes they do not speak up, but they still care. Many people avoid saying anything because they do not want to risk a fight or lose someone who might react negatively. These conversations are still necessary, especially when it comes to alcohol or drug use. We cannot suffer in silence. I have learned that the stigma of addiction helps too many people from asking for help. "Just stop" is a cruel phrase that dismisses the war going on inside our minds. Breaking addiction is not easy, and it is never just willpower. It's the daily decision to fight back and believe that life can be better than being stuck in the bottle.

Relapse does not mean failure. It means the battle isn't over yet. Every time I slipped, I learned something new about myself and about the triggers that pulled me back in. The most important thing I realized is that progress is not lost when I stumble; it stops when I give up. Healing isn't a straight path, but every step from rock bottom counts — even the tiniest of steps matter.

REFLECTION:

Relapse forced me to face the truth that recovery is not a straight line but a lifelong process of falling, learning, and standing again. It is not a weakness to stumble; it is human. I used to think relapse meant I had failed, that everything I had worked for disappeared the moment I picked up another drink. What I have come to understand is that relapse does not erase progress. It exposes the places that still hurt, the emotions I tried to bury, and the parts of myself I still need to understand. Every time I went back to drinking, it started long before I ever touched a bottle. It started with the silence I let grow too loud, the pressure I refused to share, and the pain I tried to handle alone. I used to drink to quiet the noise in my head, but the truth is, the silence afterward was louder. The hardest part of relapse is not stopping again; it is forgiving yourself long enough to try. I had to learn that progress is not erased by a single mistake, and that getting back up matters more than how far I fell. There is no shame in starting over. The only absolute failure is deciding that you are not worth another chance. What keeps me going now is knowing that I am not defined by the days I slipped, but by the strength it took to rise again. Healing is not about perfection. It is about persistence. Every day I stay sober, I prove that I am still choosing life, still choosing honesty, and still choosing to believe that even after relapse, there is hope.

READER'S REFLECTION:

1. What does relapse mean to you when you look beyond the shame or guilt?
2. When did you first realize that healing would not be a straight line?
3. What emotions or events tend to lead you back to old habits?
4. What did you learn about yourself the last time you fell and got back up?
5. Who have you pushed away in moments of struggle, and what can you do to improve that response?
6. What would progress look like if you stopped measuring it by perfection?
7. What do you need more of right now, support, rest, honesty, or forgiveness, and how would that help?

Control the Controllables

Different stages of life come with various kinds of worry. When I was younger, I was afraid of the future. As I have gotten older, I have caught myself worrying more about the inevitable. Fate is decided, but destiny is chosen. I had that tattooed on me to remind myself that my DNA and genetics control part of my timeline, but I still get the opportunity to provide what I do to the mix. It reminds me that I am responsible for my life. The decisions I make shape everything. I cannot waste time worrying about a future that has not happened yet. The only thing I can do is set myself up for success. As I stated before, it is a long life, and I control the time between the dash on my tombstone. There is a catch to that statement. Life will still throw things at me that I did not cause nor could control.

When I was in high school, I lived about ten miles from school in the country. That was a brutal 45-minute bus ride every day. Getting my driver's license and not having to take that bus felt like winning the lottery. One morning, I was getting ready for school when a classmate called to say she was running late. She asked me to pick up her friend. I was also running late and told her I would not be able to. On that occasion, it felt like a simple decision. I had no idea what it would mean later. Being late would have been a lot better than not showing up at all. I went to school, went about my day, and did not think much more about it. Around the fourth period, I found out they had been in an accident. I visited the driver in the hospital; sadly, the passenger did not make it.

That has stayed with me for years. Both she and I influenced that passenger's life. If I had gone to pick her up, she would most likely still be alive.

The timing might have changed. The snowplow turning might have changed. Something would have been different. Instead, the driver picked her up and, in a rush, started speeding. Our family farm was about a quarter mile from where the accident happened. She drove past the farm, came up to a snowplow, and tried to pass it in a no-passing zone. The snowplow turned left, and it nearly cut the car in half. The passenger died on impact. The driver walked away with lacerations and a few broken bones. She survived, but that day followed her for years.

I also carried my own guilt. I told myself that if I had not been so selfish, the passenger might still be alive. All three of us had choices in that moment that could have led to different outcomes. Her driving and her decisions were beyond my control, but I still felt like I had failed the deceased passenger. The driver and I were both worried about the same thing that morning. Being late. That worry led us to make bad decisions. If she had not rushed, suppose I had agreed to pick up the friend. If either of us had accepted being late and slowed down, then that could have affected the outcome. Every time I go to the farm, I see the cross and the teddy bear at the crash site. They are still there, even now, twenty-eight years later at the time of writing this.

This is an extreme example, but it reminds me of something important. I cannot spend my life terrified of every possible future event, or I would never leave the house. The only real option is to control what I can control. I cannot control the future. I can only take steps that move in the direction I want to go. The passenger's future ended that day. Ours did not. If I threw my hands up and decided that nothing was worth planning for, I would never get anywhere. I still have to take responsibility for the decisions I can make. That is the only way I will ever reach my destinations ahead of me.

One of the biggest things I can control is my happiness. What makes me happy? My wife, my career, and the things I have worked hard to build are near the top. I am proud of my education. I am proud of how I pushed through situations that trap many people in misery and drive them to give up. I chose to stay positive despite the negative influences surrounding me. It is easy to blame other people for where my life went off the rails. I did that for years. The truth is that my mistakes are mine. Even if someone else had a hand in them, I have to own my part. That is one of the first fundamental steps in self-awareness. Accountability.

For a long time, I relied on blaming others as a built-in excuse to allow my failures. It was a convenient way to avoid looking in the mirror. I fell into that trap early in my adult life. I did not do myself any favors until I took a hard look at my life and asked what I actually wanted out of it. At the time, I had a dead-end job and was in a relationship with someone who had no real ambition. Some people are okay with that. I was not.

The person I was dating lived in my house with her young daughter. I was paying all the bills and helping raise someone else's kid, while her ex did not pay child support. I was working over forty hours a week at my day job and bartending on Friday and Saturday nights. Her mom ran a daycare and was willing to watch her daughter for free, but my girlfriend at the time chose to work part-time instead. It is a problem when your paycheck for two weeks is for four hours of work, and you are okay with it. She did not want a relationship. She wanted a free ride. Some people are OK with being the one who carries everything. I am not that person.

I stayed in that relationship because I did not want to feel alone. One night, I came home from bartending and lay in bed next to her. I started dozing off when I heard her phone ding from an incoming text. When I opened my eyes and looked at her, she pulled the phone from her chest to the far side of her body, away from me. When someone does that, they are usually hiding something they do not want you to see. I asked to see the phone. She said no. I told her that if she would not show me, she needed to leave. She got out of bed and started packing. I followed her around the house and kept asking to see the messages. She kept walking and kept avoiding the question.

I eventually gave up and went back to the bedroom. She made a mistake and left the phone on the nightstand. I am not someone who likes going through other people's stuff, but I picked it up and read what I needed. There was a message that said, "I wish you were here in bed next to me," and a reply that said, "Me too." My heart sank, but I was not surprised. I knew something was going on. That was my clarity. I ended the relationship and had them move out.

After that, I became a lot more selective about who I let into my life. I decided I would rather be alone than feel that way again. No matter what you do, there is always risk. You might find someone who feels like their person, and it might still end. You cannot control that, only yourself. You cannot control someone else's emotions, their responses, or whether they stay. If I spend all my time worrying about that and about the future, I will never be present in my own life. I will hesitate to go after things that might be good for me because I am afraid of being hurt. At some point, is it even worth the risk? Do we want similar things in life? Will this person stand in the fire with me when things get hard, or will they run?

There was a time when I was working a solid union job. Good pay. Good stability. Then the company announced it was moving to Texas. I had just enrolled in school. I visited another company that aligned with my field of study. After owning a house for a few years, the last thing I wanted was a pay cut, but that is precisely what I took. I went from $27 an hour down to $12.50. That hurt. I got raises quickly, but I was still nowhere near what I had been making. It would have been easy to use that as an excuse to quit school, to say it was not the right time, and settle. Instead, I kept going.

I pushed through school while working full-time. After earning my bachelor's degree, I landed a better-paying job, but it still was not where I wanted to be. I kept going and finished my master's degree. That led to a role as a Business Development Manager. I traveled around the United States, Europe, and India. I saw different cultures and met people from all over. I gave international presentations on design software. It was an incredible experience, but the travel was heavy, and Bonnie and I were planning our wedding. I found a great opportunity as a middle manager overseeing a couple of departments, and made the change.

Fast forward a few more years. An outbreak hits. We built a new house. In eight years, things went from tight and stressful to stable and comfortable. I married my wife and continued to grow within the organization. The VP told me I was the next executive in line for the company, but that's in the future. I do not sit around worrying about whether it will or when it will happen. I have no control over that decision. All I can do is keep doing my best work.

The right opportunity will show up, whether it is there or somewhere else.

I actually appreciate the struggle now. It forced me to develop resolve, perseverance, and determination. It reminded me that I have worth and a purpose. When I was younger, I did not see that. I did not know what my purpose was. Most of us do not grow up with business owners for parents or come from wealthy families. We do not have someone else's fortune waiting to carry us. We cannot depend on someone else to build our lives for us. Everyone is busy chasing their own dreams.

I went back to school after being kicked out the first time for poor grades. I could have stopped there and told myself it just was not meant to be. The truth was that my priorities were not aligned with my goals. I was young and thought I knew everything. Alcohol and a fraternity took over more space than my future did. That could have been my excuse for the rest of my life. Something inside me refused to let that be the end of the story. I had a hunger to do something more with my life. Maybe it came from how I grew up. Perhaps it was because I knew no one else would do it for me.

Whatever the reason, I passed up many opportunities to quit. There were plenty of moments where it would have been easier to fall than to get back up. I almost did at one point, but I forced myself to keep moving. Sometimes we have to dig deeper than we think is possible. We may not get the promotion, the grade, or the relationship we were aiming for. That does not mean we stop. The only time we really lose is when we stop trying. The only exception is chasing someone who clearly does not want a relationship. We cannot force someone to love us or build feelings out of thin air. That fight is not worth it, as others will see the value.

Life will always throw challenges at us. Some are within reach. Some are not. The secret is learning the difference. When I stop wasting energy trying to control things that were never mine to control, I free up energy to focus on what actually matters. I can control my effort. I can control my attitude. I can control my choices and how I respond when things do not go my way. Those small acts of control add up. They build resilience and self-respect.

When I focus on what is in my power and let the rest go, the things I used to fear start to lose their grip. Worry gets a little quieter. Purpose starts to feel more real. That is what it means to control the controllables. It is not about pretending life is fair. It is about owning my part in it and choosing my next step, even when I do not know exactly where the road leads.

REFLECTION:

When I think about controlling the controllables, I keep coming back to how much time I used to spend trying to manage everything but myself. I tried to control outcomes, other people's choices, and even how they felt about me, as if I could somehow bend life into the shape I wanted by sheer force. All it ever did was exhaust me and leave me angry at things I never had power over in the first place. The stories in this chapter are reminders that my real power has always been in the decisions I make, the standards I set, and the boundaries I hold. I cannot change the past, I cannot rewrite what other people did, and I cannot save anyone who is no longer with us. I can choose how I respond, what I tolerate, and how hard I am willing to work for the life I want. Letting go of what I cannot control is not surrender. It is freedom. It gives me the space to focus on what matters most. My effort. My attitude. My growth. My integrity. That is where my life actually changes, one decision at a time.

READER'S REFLECTION:

1. Where in your life are you trying to control things that are clearly outside your control?
2. What are the parts of your current situation that are yours to own and change?
3. How much time do you spend replaying the past or worrying about the future instead of taking one small step now?
4. Is there a relationship, job, or habit you are staying in out of fear instead of because it supports the life you want?
5. What excuses do you catch yourself using that protect you from discomfort but keep you stuck?
6. If you focused only on your effort, your attitude, and your next decision,

what would look different this week?

Stop Being Self-Critical

This is a lesson I wish I had learned earlier in life. For a long time, I used my past as a measuring stick instead of a teacher. I was my own harshest critic, and no one judged me as harshly as I judged myself. I carried a negative self-image even though, on the surface, I appeared upbeat. The only time that slipped was during my struggles with alcohol and the consequences that came with it. It took time and honesty to face my demons, but no one else could do that work for me. I had to take the negative parts of my story and use them to build something better. Every day is a new chance to begin again, and opportunities are always around if we are willing to see them.

Mistakes are part of being human. They set us back, but they also teach us. There were times when I would replay old mistakes in my mind, dissecting every decision until it hurt to think about them. One day, I realized I was spending more time criticizing myself than living. That moment forced me to stop and ask what all that guilt was really doing for me. The answer was nothing. Letting go of that constant self-judgment gave me room to breathe again. Being hard on myself over them never helped. I made choices that did not always lead where I expected, like taking a massive pay cut to pursue a career that matched my education. That decision was difficult, but it changed the direction of my life. Would things have turned out better or worse if I had not made that leap? I will never know. What I do know is that the risk helped me grow. The lessons that came from that discomfort shaped who I am today. Even now, I sometimes feel like I am not where I want to be, but that drive keeps me moving forward. Maybe it is chasing rainbows, but I would rather dream too big than stop dreaming altogether.

I chose education and career over having children. For some, that might seem unthinkable, and for others, it might make perfect sense. What matters is being at peace with the path you choose. I have learned that doubt and self-criticism can stop progress before it even begins. When I make big decisions, I take time to carefully think them through. I often use a pros and cons list or a SWOT analysis (Strengths, Weaknesses, Opportunities, and Threats) to look at things from every angle. Sometimes, even after that effort, I still make mistakes. If I made those choices with thought and intent, I could live with them. That is what matters most.

Failure is inevitable. I have failed many times, in school, in relationships, and even in friendships. I was not mature enough at first to handle responsibility, and I did not always put in the effort to make things last. Relationships require work, and when that effort fades, the connection begins to break down. Others have also let me down, but over time, I learned that forgiveness is far more powerful than anger. I do not want anyone living rent-free in my mind. I turn every failure into something useful. Holding on to resentment is like carrying bricks. The more bricks you hold, the heavier they become. I would set those bricks down to build a stronger foundation.

Being kind to myself is not about being complacent. It is about understanding that growth takes time and that mistakes are part of that process. Forgiving myself has created space for peace and confidence. I have started to see progress in places where I used to see only problems. Life feels less like a punishment and more like a process of learning. Each time I give myself reprieve, I move closer to the person I am meant to become.

REFLECTION:

I have always been my own harshest critic. The voice in my head could be crueler than anything anyone else could say to me. For what felt like an eternity, I thought being hard on myself was a way to stay motivated, but it only wore me down. It stripped away my confidence and left me carrying guilt that served no purpose. I am learning to replace that harshness with understanding, to treat myself with the same compassion I would offer to someone I care about. The more I do that, the easier it becomes to grow, to heal, and to move forward without the constant weight of judgment.

READER'S REFLECTION:

1. When did you first start believing that being hard on yourself was the way to improve?
2. How do you speak to yourself in moments of disappointment, and would you say those exact words to someone you love?
3. What would your day look like if you gave yourself the same patience you give others?
4. In what ways can self-compassion become a daily practice rather than a rare exception?
5. What does it mean to you to forgive yourself for simply being human?

Bad Days Are Inevitable

Wouldn't life be great without the added stress of bad days? We have all faced them. Whether it is locking your keys in the car, losing your wallet, or getting a flat tire, these moments can test your patience. They remind us that everything will not always go our way. The good news is that bad days pass, just like good ones do. When you find yourself in the middle of one, remind yourself that it will not last forever. Try to hold on to the good moments a little longer when they come around.

After we got married, Bonnie's lifelong pets all became sick and passed away within a year. Her Yorkie died of testicular cancer, and her two cats, who were brothers, passed from age-related illnesses. We had the vet come to the house to help them pass peacefully. Losing them was incredibly hard for us. While I had only known them for five years, those animals had been a source of comfort through some of her most challenging times for much longer. The last animal in the house was my Bengal, and after some time, we decided to bring home another puppy. We started attending rescue events and visiting shelters, and eventually found one we wanted to adopt. Coincidentally, Bonnie fell in love with a Yorkie puppy that cost $2,500, a price we couldn't justify. She started an online fundraising campaign to help pay for an emotional support animal, knowing it was a long shot.

We signed the adoption papers for the rescue dog. We planned to bring him home in two weeks. A few days later, Bonnie got an email saying someone had donated the full amount to her campaign, enough to get the Yorkie puppy. We were stunned. Suddenly, we had two dogs: a five-pound Yorkshire Terrier and a rescue dog — a mix of Husky, German Shepherd, and Pit Bull — expected to reach about 55 pounds. He is now 120 pounds, and the two of them get along like brothers.

The first weekend with the rescue dog went perfectly. The following Monday, we had to kennel him while we were at work since he was still getting used to the new house. I will never forget that day. I had a rough day at work and couldn't wait to come home, sit outside, and let the stress fade. When I walked through the door, I was hit with a smell that stopped me in my tracks. It was awful, a mix of vomit and feces. I followed the scent to the kennel, and he went potty in there. He ended up getting sick from the smell and spreading it everywhere in the kennel. He must have gotten nauseated by the stench and thrown up inside and outside the kennel door, and he had been in that mess for a couple of hours.

I felt bad for him more than anything. It took more than an hour to clean everything up, the kennel, the floor, and even his ears, as it was everywhere. It was one of those days you have to power through while trying not to gag. But in the middle of all that, I reminded myself that he was scared, alone, and didn't understand what was happening. I couldn't get angry at him. After that day, he never had another accident in the house, and within a month, we stopped kenneling him completely.

It takes time to build trust, whether it is with animals or people. We don't have children, so our pets fill the home with energy and love. I know that someday, we will face the pain of losing them, just like we did before. But that is the trade-off for loving anything deeply. It is temporary. So, I remind myself to appreciate every good day we have with them, to hold on to the joy, because those memories help us get through the hard times.

Bad days remind us that we are human. They test our patience, our attitude, and our ability to stay calm when everything feels out of control. The key is not to avoid them, but to let them pass without losing who we are in the process. Every time we handle a setback with patience instead of anger, we grow a little stronger. Bad days will always come and go, but the strength we build from them will stay with us for life.

REFLECTION:

No matter how strong or positive I try to be, bad days still happen. Struggles, disappointments, and setbacks are simply part of being alive. The goal is not to avoid them, but to face them without losing myself in the frustration. I have learned that bad days do not define who I am. They test my patience and perspective, but they also remind me that I am still standing. What matters most is how I respond. I can let the day break me down, or I can take a breath and remember that it will pass. Every bad day ends, and when tomorrow comes, I get another chance to begin again. I always try to remember that my bad day may be nowhere near as bad as someone else's.

READER'S REFLECTION:

1. When you're having a bad day, how do you usually treat yourself or others? What could you do differently?
2. What helps you remember that one bad day doesn't define your entire story?
3. How do you balance allowing yourself to feel pain without letting it consume you?
4. What simple actions or rituals help you reset when everything feels heavy?
5. What could it mean to see bad days as part of healing instead of proof of failure?

An Honest Self-Assessment

The human ego can sometimes interfere with our subconscious and how we present ourselves to others. This disconnect can harm relationships due to internal conflict. In life, you will most likely never fully align with everyone, as each person has their own perspectives and experiences. This is not necessarily a bad thing, but it can negatively impact self-reflection and stunt our personal growth. As a person, you need to want to change for the better, but if you don't recognize a problem, you will thwart your own efforts. This may occur naturally as we age, or it may happen more when you shift from a doer to a thinker mindset. I have also spent more time as a coach and mentor, which has put my own journey into perspective. I spend more time on self-reflection now than I ever did before. It is not a requirement in life, but we all can improve something, no matter who we are.

There are many tools you can use to discover who you are, but you must answer honestly and be true to yourself when using them. We all have strengths and shortcomings, and need to be sincere. There are many tools available for self-assessment, or you can opt to take an assessment with a professional. You can take the Myers–Briggs test, Enneagram Personality Test, Eysenck Personality Questionnaire, the HEXACO Model of Personality Structure Personality Inventory, among many others.

I took the Myers–Briggs personality test and found that I am an INTJ, which is a relatively accurate result. Below is a brief overview of me and how these items are thought to function, with a fair degree of accuracy. Does this mean something bad if you are one or the other? Not at all. It gives you a little more definition of who you are. I would recommend taking a test to establish a baseline of your current state, if you haven't already. I know they do this in schools, and maybe you already know your personality type. Here are my results, along with some insight into myself.

I - is for Introvert.

As I stated in previous chapters, I moved around quite a bit, and it takes some time to develop a comfort level when learning to speak in my voice. It was always a new group. I recall that in school, I was terrified of giving a demonstrative speech. It was an easy subject because I loved to fish, and my presentation showed how to tie a fishing knot. I ended up saying I wasn't ready even though I had everything I needed for the presentation. The teacher allowed me to give the presentation to an empty class after school. It may or may not have hindered my growth, but at the time, I appreciated it. It took many attempts at public speaking, and everyone could see that I was extremely nervous and very uncomfortable when forced out of my comfort zone. It took repeated opportunities to get up and talk in front of people to become comfortable, and I still get nervous.

N - is for Intuitive.

I view things from a broad perspective. I have always questioned everything and have been inquisitive about what can be viewed from a 30,000-foot perspective. We sometimes get hung up on a single point or data set and fail to consider the broader context. On the other hand, I sometimes don't get granular enough and need help from others to see the finer details. Both provide value, and neither is wrong, but it is good to ensure I keep it in check and don't forget the details. I like to think outside the box and imagine what can be. If we all just did as we were told, innovation wouldn't be at the forefront of our imaginations. At times, we get a sneaking suspicion, or our intuition kicks in, allowing us to make a decision from the gut instead of the mind. That can also lead us into trouble if we do not fully understand the choice.

T - is for Thinking.

I agree with being a thinker. I like to learn. It can be a downfall because I want to understand how things work, rather than just using something. Some people don't care how it works as long as it does. That's not me. To understand, I like to investigate and see how and why. That is one of the reasons I went to school in my mid-twenties. First, the thirst for knowledge, and second, the realization that without an education, you have a ceiling of limitations. I didn't make the rules; society did. I am not advocating spending your life learning and incurring significant expenses to educate yourself. You can have a great life by pursuing a career in the trades. You can even head to the library or take courses on Coursiv or Udemy online. If you want to be inquisitive, you have more at your fingertips than the generation before you, and they had more than the generation before them. Could you imagine an encyclopedia salesman coming to your door trying to sell you a set in this day and age? That is what you had for the times. Television was still in its infancy when our grandparents were young. Constant exposure to instant information makes it hard to distinguish between fact, fiction, and propaganda.

J - is for judging.

I like structure, almost to a fault. I try to manage life to eliminate stress. I am a planner and am very structured. I still print off boarding passes and reservations just in case my phone dies while traveling. I recall a time when I flew into Cleveland, and my phone didn't have service. The rental car didn't have GPS, and none were available. It was one of my first business trips, and I learned quickly to prepare. Fail to prepare, prepare to fail. Others can go their whole life without so much as a plan and be okay with that. Unfortunately, that isn't me. Not that there is anything wrong with that. Having family in the military helped shape the structure of my life, which is why I am the way I am. I liked writing growing up because it followed rules. You create an outline (structure) and use it to move the story forward. Now the outline can change, but you still have that inherent structure.

When you do this, do not think that there is something wrong with you. It helps you figure out who you are. There are updated tests that do not categorize you into sixteen buckets like this one. Please feel free to explore and find out what type of personality you are. They use different terminology, but the outcome remains the same. You receive a breakdown that can help you identify your strengths and opportunities. Notice I didn't say weaknesses. Our differences are not weaknesses; they help us on our own individual paths. I know I could never go on stage in front of thousands of people. I can, however, write and tell stories without issue. I hope my honesty and vulnerability come through. I hope these stories are helpful to you.

Taking an honest look at oneself is one of the most awkward things one will ever do, but it is also one of the most freeing. When we understand who we are, we stop trying to be who everyone else expects us to be. We learn to work with our strengths rather than hiding our flaws. Self-awareness is not about perfection; it is about progress. The more honest we are with ourselves, the more we open the door to growth, purpose, and peace.

REFLECTION:

Taking an honest look at myself was not easy. It meant facing parts of me that I had ignored or explained away for years. I used to think self-awareness was about fixing what was wrong, but now I see it as learning who I am and how I respond to the world. The more honest I am about my strengths and flaws, the more peace I find in knowing where I stand. It is not about becoming perfect. It is about understanding myself enough to keep growing. I have learned that self-reflection is not a one-time event. It is a lifelong process that shapes how I show up for myself and the people around me.

READER'S REFLECTION:

1. When was the last time you truly paused to evaluate where you are and not with judgment, but with honesty?
2. What truths about yourself have you been avoiding because they're uncomfortable to face?
3. How do you usually react to your own flaws, with curiosity or criticism?
4. What strengths have you overlooked because you've been too focused on what's wrong?
5. What would it look like to see yourself clearly and still choose kindness?
6. Have you done a self-assessment? Were you surprised by the results?

Overcoming Our Pasts for a Better Future

A past. That is the one place you cannot and do not want to live, but it seems like most of us end up there anyway. I lived there for a long time. It was familiar and comfortable, even when it was painful. I blamed people for how my life turned out and used that blame as the reason I could not grow. It felt justified at the time, but it only gave me a built-in excuse to fail. I know that because I used it. When you look back, you already know the outcome. It is like looking in the rearview mirror. You see what is behind you, but you cannot change it.

There are stories of people who rise from the ashes like a phoenix, but there are also stories where people never escape the weight of what happened to them. Some numb their pain through addiction. Others stay in abusive situations because it is all they have known. My wife and I are both works in progress. Middle-aged or not, life still throws punches and knocks us down. The truth is simple. We can stay down on the canvas, or we can get back up. The past should be used as a lesson, not a life sentence. We may have to claw our way out of bad situations, but when we do, that effort becomes the foundation for a stronger future. I have lost people to addiction, and I know people who survived — the same goes for domestic violence. A downward spiral can happen fast. Faster than you ever expect.

I will never forget the panic attack I had in my late teens. I had never experienced anything like it. I was driving home from a friend's house when my heart suddenly started racing. My face flushed, I started sweating, and my mind spun into complete panic. Nothing triggered it. Looking back, maybe it was the pack of cigarettes I smoked or the ridiculous amount of soda I drank, but at the time, it felt like something was seriously wrong. I went to the doctor, and after a short conversation, she prescribed Paxil. Giving a teenage kid a powerful SSRI while he is already drowning in hormones is unbelievable to me now. The medication made me depressed, and the sexual side effects hit hard. They lasted long after I stopped taking it. It was one of the reasons I was still a virgin at nineteen.

Imagine being in your prime and questioning whether your body will work at all. The reality was that it did not. You can put in all the effort in the world, but you are not going to win that fight. After that happens a few times, doubt becomes your shadow. Being naked becomes a source of anxiety instead of something natural. I was never comfortable in my own skin back then, as it was. The truth is, we only get one body to live in. The sooner we accept that, the better. Even the most attractive people deal with insecurities. As kids, we are constantly compared to each other. Then the media steps in and shows us edited, airbrushed, and photoshopped versions of beauty that humans can't achieve. No wonder so many of us grow up feeling inadequate.

If you have dealt with the side effects from pharmaceutical drugs, I feel for you. I would not wish that experience on anyone. They can wreak havoc on your body and mind. I do not believe the system has our best interests at heart. Drug reps show up looking polished with their miracle cure, and suddenly that pill becomes the answer for millions. Then come the side effects. Crying spells, breast tenderness, stomach issues, thinning hair, and reproductive problems. I am not a medical professional. I am sharing my experience and my opinion. Antidepressants and antianxiety medications get handed out like candy, and many people do not realize the long-term cost until they are living it.

The truth is that many people are not only dealing with emotional pain. They are running around with vitamin and nutrient deficiencies that no one ever checked for. Things like a good multivitamin, B complex, magnesium, potassium, vitamin D, and K, or fish oil can help some people. Then there are supplements like 5-HTP, which can increase serotonin, but those can be dangerous if combined with medications. That is why working with a doctor you trust matters. Get blood work done. Ask questions. Push for answers.

Most clinics do not routinely check for deficiencies unless you ask. It can be expensive, but so can adding prescription after prescription in a never-ending cycle.

I have seen that cycle more than once. One medication leads to another to manage the side effects of the first. Dry mouth and cracked skin become another pill. Kidney concerns become another. The list grows. Your quality of life shrinks. It took years for my wife's blood pressure to stabilize. Years of living in constant fight-or-flight. Her blood pressure hit 234 over 126 and landed her in the ICU for five days. A kidney specialist happened to be working that night and took her case seriously. Within a month, her blood pressure was normal, and more than half her medications had been discontinued. That experience showed me how broken parts of the healthcare system are and how important it is to advocate for yourself.

It took both of us a long time to move past our pasts truly. My wife once swore she would join a convent before ever dating again. That should tell you what her understanding of love had become. She thought love was pain, fear, and survival because that was all she had known. Narcissists isolate, control, gaslight, and manipulate. They convince you that you are the problem when it is really them. Love should never make you feel small or afraid. Yes, relationships have bumps in the road, but they should never cause harm. The only time love should hurt is when you are grieving someone you lost. That grief is the measure of what they meant to you. Anything else is not love.

Our pasts leave scars, but those scars prove we survived. They remind us of how far we have come. For years, I tried to hide my trauma and assumed that others knew better than I did. Real healing began when I took responsibility for my own well-being. Getting second opinions, researching, learning, and trusting my instincts changed everything. Understanding my history gave me power I had never felt before. Moving forward is not about pretending the past never happened. It is about learning enough from it that it no longer runs the show. When you reach that point, you stop reliving your past. You finally start living your life.

REFLECTION:

The past can feel like a weight chained to our ankles, dragging us back every time we try to move forward. However, the truth is that we are not defined by what has happened to us. We are defined by what we do with it. For most of my life, I carried my past like it was proof of who I was. Every mistake, every failure, every wound became part of my identity. It took years to understand that the past isn't meant to be lived in; it's meant to be learned from. Letting go didn't happen overnight. It took time, honesty, and the willingness to stop running from my own story. The hardest part wasn't forgiving others; it was forgiving myself. Once I did, I finally felt free. My past didn't disappear; it just stopped defining me. Now, it's simply the ground I stand on, not the weight I am carrying.

READER'S REFLECTION:

1. What parts of your past still weigh you down, even when you thought you'd moved on?
2. How has your pain shaped the person you've become, in both good and difficult ways?
3. What stories from your past need to be rewritten from a place of understanding rather than regret?
4. Who do you need to forgive, or what do you need to release, to move forward freely?
5. What would it look like to stop running from your past and start learning from it instead?

Excuses Are Like Assholes

Like the old saying goes, excuses are like assholes, and everyone has one. I know that because I spent years perfecting mine. I hear excuses slide into everyday conversations, even when people don't realize they are doing it. Someone will say something like, "I didn't go to the work party because I was exhausted and didn't want to go." That kind of justification slips out before they even think about it. We all do that sometimes. The truth is simple. The only person I need to justify my actions to is myself, unless in a relationship, then communication and justification definitely matter. Otherwise, the other side of the bed can feel bigger and colder than it used to.

I used to carry around a built-in excuse for every failure. Living that way made it easy to accept defeat before I even tried. I am not talking about minor things like skipping a work party. I am talking about bigger choices, the kind that change the course of a life. I didn't believe in myself. I didn't think I was worth much, and I let that belief become my excuse every time I fell short. I repeated that cycle when I smoked, when I wasted money drinking and partying, and even when I stalled out in my career. One of the tools that helped me the most was setting tangible goals and following through. I held myself accountable. Setting a goal to win the lottery isn't a goal. It has to be something achievable that I am willing to pursue. When I look at it through a project management lens, goals are simply personal projects I expect myself to complete.

I had an entire list of excuses about why I couldn't quit smoking. Stress, work, and the need to relax were the three I used most. Quitting smoking is not easy for anyone. It took me three attempts. The first two tries were half-planned, half-hearted, and honestly destined to fail. I just tried not to smoke and hoped for the best. The third attempt was different. I built an actual plan. First, I set a quit date. As that date came closer, I stripped my environment of anything connected to smoking. I tossed lighters, cleaned out ashtrays, and wiped down every place where the smell lingered. I wanted no reminders.

The day before my quit date, I bought a couple of weeks' worth of gum and a pack of cigarettes I didn't even like, for work, just in case. I threw out the brand I used to smoke. I broke each cigarette at the filter, tossed the filters in the garbage, and pushed the rest down the garbage disposal. I did that so I couldn't dig the paper wrapper with the tobacco out of the trash and patch them back together, to smoke them. I think most people who were broke and out of cigarettes know what I mean and have done the same. I am not proud of this, but when I was a kid, I used to check all of the outdoor business ashtrays with friends and find mostly whole cigarettes to smoke. Thinking about it now turns the stomach a bit.

On the day I quit, I carried the pack I disliked. That part might not work for everyone, but I needed it. It gave me a sense of control. I quit on my terms. It made me proud that I resisted every urge, even though I had cigarettes on me all day. I could have smoked one at any point, but I didn't. That was the moment I knew I was actually done.

Some people do better tapering off with gum or patches. I tried that route, but it kept nicotine in my system, and once the gum or patch wore off, so did the willpower. Like everything else, success comes from commitment and consistency. The first few days are hell, but it gets better. I had to stop talking to a couple of people who smoked, and I avoided places where people gathered to smoke. I also stayed away from alcohol for a bit because drinking and smoking go hand in hand.

Most goals are more manageable than quitting smoking. You set an end date and list the steps from start to finish. You check them off as you complete each one. If the end date comes and the goal isn't complete, I don't quit. I adjust the plan. If there is a roadblock, I find a way to remove it. If a step feels too large, I break it into smaller ones.

Excuses offer short-term comfort, but they steal long-term progress. The moment I stopped justifying why I couldn't do something, I started finding reasons why I could. Real change begins the second I take ownership of my choices and hold myself accountable. It doesn't matter how many times I failed before. What matters is that I stopped hiding behind the same story. When I stopped making excuses, I finally permitted myself to succeed.

REFLECTION:

For a long time, I was my own roadblock. I told myself stories that made failure easier to accept and created excuses that sounded reasonable enough to believe. It took years to realize that those justifications were not protecting me; they were keeping me stuck. Every time I explained away my choices, I gave up a piece of control over my own life. The turning point came when I stopped defending my inaction and started owning my decisions, both the good and the bad. Accountability did not make life easier, but it made it real. Once I stopped making excuses, I began to see progress where I had only seen obstacles. Growth came when I faced the truth and kept moving forward, even when it was uncomfortable.

READER'S REFLECTION:

1. What excuses do you find yourself repeating when fear or doubt shows up?
2. How often do you trade your goals for comfort or familiarity?
3. What would your life look like if you stopped waiting for the "right time" and just started?
4. When you think about accountability, what does that mean for you personally?
5. What's one small step you could take today to move closer to what you keep postponing?

Plan Things Out

Buying a house is a process that takes planning and patience. It involves several steps that depend on preparation, timing, and a clear goal. A stable job, a down payment, and a realistic understanding of monthly expenses form the foundation. Getting pre-approved for a loan helps define a price range and provides direction. Once a target amount is set, it becomes easier to search for homes within budget. From there, the decision to work with a realtor or contact a homeowner directly depends on how the property is listed. An inspection helps identify issues, and the results determine whether to move forward with an offer or negotiate further.

Checklist to Buy a Starter Home

1. Talk with a mortgage loan officer.
2. Establish a budget for a house.
3. Estimate a budget of $70,000 to $100,000 for a starter home.
4. Save for a 20% down payment to avoid paying Private Mortgage Insurance (PMI).
5. Current savings: $5,000.
6. How many months will it take to save enough to reach my goal?
7. Get pre-approved for a dollar amount greater than what you want to spend, but still within your budget.
8. Start looking at houses that are for sale.
9. Find one worth buying.

10. Talk with the realtor.
11. Submit an offer contingent upon a satisfactory inspection.
12. Did the inspection pass?
    a. Yes
    b. No (have seller fix items or accept items and give a lower offer).
13. Accept the offer or counteroffer.
14. Get the date for closing.
15. Close on the house and sign all of the paperwork.
16. Plan to move in after closing.
17. Arrange a U-Haul or helpers for the move.

The list above is only an example. Every situation will vary. It is common to start the process expecting one outcome, then adjust based on finances or timing. A plan for a $100,000 home might be revised to allow more time for a larger down payment, such as 20%. Saving $500 per month would require 30 months to reach the goal. Add that $15,000 to your $5,000 in your savings, and that would be $20,000 for your down payment. Progress is still progress. Don't be discouraged if that seems like a long time or a large amount. The loan officer or mortgage broker will help with options. First-home purchasers also have some government-backed options.

When I bought my first home, it cost $89,000, and I made a three percent down payment. Before reaching that point, I had to rebuild my credit, which delayed my timeline by several months. I also moved back home for a short time to save money. It was not an easy step, but it allowed me to refocus and strengthen my financial position.

Planning creates direction, but it does not guarantee a smooth path. Life always adds detours and delays that were never part of the original plan. The key is flexibility. Adjusting the timeline is not a failure; it is part of progress. Adding new steps, revising goals, or starting again does not erase the effort already made. Every step forward, no matter how small, builds momentum.

Planning things out gives structure and purpose. It brings clarity during uncertain times and creates measurable progress toward any goal. Life rarely unfolds exactly as expected, but having a plan in place ensures that forward motion never stops, even when detours appear. Over time, each completed step becomes a reminder of resilience and growth. The act of planning keeps momentum alive and creates a sense of control in a world that often feels unpredictable. Careful preparation will never eliminate risk, but it transforms uncertainty into direction. Every plan that takes shape becomes proof that progress is possible, even when the path ahead is uneven.

REFLECTION:

Living without a plan once felt like freedom to me, but it often led to frustration and wasted effort. Planning is not about predicting every detail of the future; it is about setting intentions and creating direction. A plan provides a map, a sense of focus, and the structure needed to handle challenges as they come. It reminds me that discipline and preparation are acts of self-respect, not restriction. Each plan, no matter how small, becomes a way to show up for myself and move closer to the life I want, rather than leaving it to chance.

READER'S REFLECTION:

1. How often do you take time to plan with intention instead of reacting to life as it comes?
2. What goals or dreams have stayed stuck in your mind because they were never written down?
3. How does structure or routine help you feel grounded and confident?
4. When has flexibility been just as important as having a plan?
5. What would it look like to plan your days around your values, not just your obligations?

No One Will Do It for Me

I learned early on that no one is going to live my life for me. It is a dog-eat-dog world, and expecting people to step in without something in return is a quick way to stay disappointed. That applies to almost anything in life. I once had a coworker I believed was solid, and I helped him land a Project Manager role at the company where I worked. A few months later, I wanted to shift positions and cut back on travel, but the person I supported did not want me anywhere near his lane. I found out later that he saw me as a threat and kept bad-talking me behind closed doors. I took a different role and had already settled in somewhere else. In my current role, I conduct more interviews than I care to count, and it is shocking how often references turn out to be the very reason someone does not get hired. Some places have even stopped asking for references because of that. Trusting the wrong person can cost one's opportunities without even realizing it. Life is already hard enough. I do not want anyone sabotaging my efforts from the shadows. I would rather tell someone no than give them a bad reference, but some people take pleasure in watching someone else stumble.

Self-motivation is something each of us chooses to build at our own pace. Some people wake up with it. Others fight like hell to keep it alive. If real change is needed in my life, I have to make it. Asking someone else to make that change for me puts pressure on them that does not belong there. Sometimes they will try to help, especially when something addictive is involved, but it strains the relationship. Placing that responsibility on someone else is not fair. They can cheer from the sidelines, but they cannot control my hands. Those hands are my actions, my choices, and my consequences. I decide what I do with them, not the other way around.

I view self-motivation the same way I do as drive. Everything starts with inputs that eventually lead to an output. If I want to drop twenty-five pounds, I know there are multiple inputs. I need a plan to reduce calories, burn fat, and stick to a routine. There are medical shortcuts, but relying on them is a dangerous mindset. The better path is a lifestyle shift, an exercise routine, and a commitment to that consistency. Like everything else, shortcuts only get someone locked in a basement in a horror movie. Avoid them. Set the plan and follow it. Setbacks happen. Injuries happen. The body does not always cooperate. Starting again is sometimes more complicated than working at a lower capacity. Any long-distance runner will confirm that endurance disappears fast. Sometimes modifications keep a person moving. Sometimes they do not. The mission is the same: get back to it as soon as possible. Quitting is easy. Fighting for motivation takes true grit.

Careers work the same way. Rejection can happen a hundred times in a row, but the next attempt might be the one that changes everything. The important thing is to hold on to the belief that something is around the corner. Feeling defeated is normal, but staying down is optional. Sometimes the next step forward is simple. Take a class. Ask for training. Tell leadership what I want. I have learned that employers are not mind readers. Communicating ambition can open doors that no one mentioned before. The mindset of "it is not my job" is the fastest way to stall out. There is a difference between being used and stepping up with intention. Some people will always take advantage of those who do everything they're asked. Over time, experience makes the line between the two easier to see.

At the end of the day, my life is my responsibility. No one is going to hand me success, happiness, or purpose. I have to build those things myself, choice by choice. The people in my life can support me, but they cannot live my life for me. Once I accepted that truth, everything shifted. I stopped waiting for the perfect opportunity and started creating it. That is when real progress began. That is when I realized the person I had been waiting for was me all along.

REFLECTION:

For a long time, I waited for someone else to step in and make things better. The truth is, no one was ever going to save me, and realizing that was one of the most freeing moments of my life. Everything I wanted, including growth, healing, and peace, was already within reach. I just had to take responsibility for it. Support systems can help, and I am grateful for those who stood beside me, but no one could walk my path for me. Real progress came when I stopped waiting for the right time or the right circumstances and started moving forward with what I had. Taking ownership of my journey meant facing hard truths, forgetting past failures, and finding strength in the effort itself. Each step taught me something new about who I am and what I am capable of. I learned that self-reliance is not about isolation but about trusting myself enough to take control of my life. The moment I stopped waiting and started acting for myself was when I truly began to live.

READER'S REFLECTION:

1. What goals or changes have you been waiting for someone else to make happen for you?
2. When did you realize that no help was coming to help you with something in life, and what did you do to remedy that?
3. How do you motivate yourself when the only person who can move things forward is you?
4. What does personal responsibility mean to you when it comes to your own growth?
5. What's one area of your life where you can stop waiting and start doing today?

Play Stupid Games Win Stupid Prizes

S ome people receive positive affirmations from their parents; I only had one parent, and she was busy trying to put a roof over our heads and food on the table. Being from a broken home creates enough challenges on its own. Self-confidence takes a significant hit when you see that your life is different than most of those around you who have two parents in their lives. At least it did for me. I still have days when I lack confidence in myself. I have a fantastic support system, including my mom, stepdad, wife, friends, and coworkers. I would highly recommend finding good people you can trust and with whom you feel comfortable discussing anything. I recollect the first time I told my mom about the drugs I did when I was in middle school. Nothing hard, just marijuana and acid. It is incredible how far things have come for the legalization of marijuana, mushroom micro-dosing, and ketamine therapies to help with addiction, depression, and overall well-being. Now, I am going to go on another tangent and tell a couple of acid and mushroom usage stories from my first times for each.

I tried acid in middle school, and yes, I said middle school, it was an experience. It was a simple white blotter acid, for those of you that aren't into that, it is a paper sheet soaked in LSD (Lysergic acid diethylamide) and dried and cut into rectangular "hits". I took one hit, cut it in half, and placed one half in my mouth. A friend of mine was with me and wanted the other half. I told him I didn't feel anything yet and that I would let him know if I needed it or not. So, after another fifteen minutes of feeling nothing, I took the second half. Now, I didn't realize it would take time to kick in. Another fifteen minutes went by, and then I started to feel the first one I had in my mouth. Everything was extremely bright, and patterns began to shift around. I thought, "Well, great, I am feeling this now, and I just took the second half."

Now, the downside is that I am the only one who's high on acid, and at this point, I have given up my right to make decisions. I had my friend guide me around as I wanted to go for a walk. I highly recommend having someone you trust for your first experience, should you choose. We went to another buddy's house, which was only two blocks, but it felt like a mile. Looking around, the houses seemed to be breathing, and you could hear every leaf rustle. It was both cool and unnerving. It was early afternoon, and we were sitting outside. They didn't want me to go inside because I was tripping. I thought what happened next was not real, but it was. As we are sitting outside, the phone rang, and I heard his mom yelling at me from the window, "It's your mom, and you have to get home. You have to go and get a haircut." The two chuckle-heads I was with broke out in full belly laughs as I turned sheet white.

Now, at the peak of the trip, I start the five-block journey home by myself. I was panicking. The walk home was a challenge, as I had to navigate through a park with a small lagoon and a bridge, and I was unsure what was real at this point. Seeing people and wildlife, it seemed like they knew I was tripping by the way they were looking at me. It could have been paranoia at this point, but I was now hyper-focused on getting home. How the hell could I have forgotten that I had a haircut appointment? On the list of hell no's, these were two of the exact scenarios that you do not want while tripping: being with someone who can take your freedom (getting grounded for doing drugs) and having someone cut your hair. Nothing like being wrapped like a burrito, forced to sit still, and having someone with a sharp instrument cut your hair while you are in a different state of mind.

After what felt like an eternity, I finally made it back home. My mind was jumbled, and as I walked up to our apartment door, I never knew how loud the covered porch was until I heard my feet pounding beneath me. I opened the door, and my mom asked me a question. I blurted out the most mish-mashed sentence I have ever sputtered. To this day, I still don't remember what came out of my mouth. She asked me, "What did you say?" I thought for a second and said, "Sorry, I forgot we had this appointment."

I went into the bathroom quickly to pee and steady my nerves. I looked in the mirror, and my pupils were *fully* dilated. I had zero color to my green eyes. I just had two enormous black circles. I never wore sunglasses, so I didn't have a pair. I had to go to my room and grab a hat to at least hide my eyes from the world, because, as I said before, the people and wildlife knew. It was quiet in the car, and I did not want to talk because of the way I threw out the last word salad as an attempt to speak. Plus, I was concentrating intensely because I now had tunnel vision, and it felt like we were traveling at warp speed. At the hair salon, everything was normal until I sat in the chair to get my hair cut. It was going fine until I twitched a bit, and she nicked my ear. My brain started focusing on it, and I perceived a flood of negative thoughts. I had to calm myself down and think hard for something good. All I could feel was the throbbing of the cut, and I felt my heart racing at that point. On a scale of 1 to 10, I would give it 0 stars and not recommend it. Things slowly went back to normal, and I was finally coming down from the trip. Normality returned, and my irises finally pulled back from the black holes they were in.

The lesson from the whole experience was that no matter what happens, I can find a way to get through any situation. This day could have been way worse. My mom could have found out and grounded me. I could have lost my composure and done something foolish. According to health class, I could have gone on a permanent trip, as the stories and rumors go about doing LSD. That was my one and only LSD experiment. That traumatized me a bit. I swore off trying any Psychedelic drugs forever.

Fast forward six years, because forever was too long for swearing things off. A friend of mine had grown mushrooms. Well, he was a friend of a friend. We attended a house party, and it was a typical gathering of late teens and early twenties until it wasn't. That friend of a friend pulled out some freshly grown mushrooms. If you have ever done anything after you have been drinking, you know it is hard to gauge the effects of the drug you are on because your perception is already nonexistent from the alcohol. You also lose track of time when you are drunk. I was probably almost through a 12-pack of beer when a full gallon-sized bag of mushrooms got put in front of me. I highly recommend never combining anything, whether it is drugs or alcohol. A typical dose is about one whole mushroom. They looked harmless enough, so I took two and a stem. I am not a patient person, and, having not learned from my last experience, I found myself repeating the same mistake. After about half an hour, I still wasn't feeling any effects, even though beer goggles clouded my judgment. My impatience got the best of me, and rather than waiting to see what might happen, I decided to take further action. This lack of patience and disregard for the lessons I should have learned from previous experiences set the stage for the events that followed.

I spoke up, "Hey, I am not feeling anything yet." The friend of a friend tossed the bag at me and said, "Suit yourself." I thought to myself, "What the hell was that supposed to mean?" So, I grabbed four more full shrooms and a large cap and proceeded to fill my face with them. Washed down the atrociously horrible-tasting mushrooms. In hindsight, this was a "hero dose" of a drug. Micro-dosing involves taking just enough to gain the benefits without experiencing side effects. A "hero dose" is the opposite. It is taking too high a dose to be sure you are in another state of mind or consciousness.

The neighbor of the house party I attended invited us over to hang out in his basement. There were like eight of us who obliged. If you have ever drunk and done another drug, your brain is going to be affected by the higher levels of intoxication. I did not know that was a thing until this very evening. The basement was located in a quad-level home, with four floors, and half flights of stairs between each level. In this basement, there was the most native American-themed room I have ever seen in my life. The bathroom wallpaper even featured Native Americans wearing headdresses. I will get back to that wallpaper in a little bit. I sat down on the couch, and everyone began to fill in the other available spots. As I look around this room, there are spears, buffalo heads, a headdress, pictures of native Americans, and even knick-knack figurines. This was the whole nine yards. I started to feel a bit funny. Something inside of me changed. I was no longer drunk. I went stone cold sober, then came on something else.

The owner turns on Enya's "Orinoco Flow" (Sail Away) at an obnoxiously loud level and puts on a headdress. To put it into perspective, everyone in that basement had one mushroom, except for one guy sitting by me, who had a couple. I, myself, was going on a completely different journey than anyone else. He tells everyone to get up. It was at this moment that I knew I was tripping, and so was everyone else. I start to laugh uncontrollably at what is going on. I asked the guy next to me, "Is that fucking Enya, and are they huddling in a circle? What the fuck is going on?" I got no response. He was seated in a fully upright position, as if he were strapped into a ride, with his hands and feet kept inside at all times.

Did I say something, or did I think it? I had to have said something because the man in the headdress gave me a sneer, and they all looked at me. I thought he said, "Look at those guys on the couch, they are not part of the tribe." After about the third or fourth time of the same song playing on repeat, and these guys in a circle, swaying and chanting. The trip from the mushrooms is intensifying. I began to feel a sensation I had never experienced before. My brain was confused about what to do. I wasn't sure if I had to vomit or poop. That happens at times with mushrooms, at least in terms of upset stomach. I had to muster all the strength I had to get off the couch with the Native American scenery cover on it.

I staggered to the bathroom. Unsure of what I had to do. I started by trying to poop. I placed my head in my hand for what felt like eternity. I couldn't go. I picked my head up, and the damn native American headdress images started flipping back and forth. I sat tripping balls. The trip was way, way worse this time than it was when I was on acid. I am not sure what level was higher than that, but this was about four or five levels above that. On a scale of one to ten, the screen read 'tilt.' I felt an urge to get sick. I was sure my body was trying to purge what's going on.

I pulled up my pants, stood up, turned around, and flushed the toilet. I then fell to my knees. I looked at the water in the commode, and it looked like a rainbow of colored bubbles. My stomach was now in knots, I started salivating, and hung my head deep in the toilet; now the bubbles were going past my peripheral vision. As my head hung down in the clean, cold porcelain, I felt the urge to purge the demons I had ingested out of my guts. The next dry heave forced out a fart. I had to think for a moment if that was poop or a fart. I was so concentrated on the task at hand that I wasn't sure of the other feeling I felt. I sat back on the toilet and checked my underwear. Thank you, Lord, for not letting me crap myself. At that point, the Indian heads were still flipping, but I was seeing more colors. I was freaking out because I didn't know what to do. I mustered up the strength to get up, pulled up my pants, and opened the door.

I thought to myself, "Is fucking Enya still playing?" My psyche was now broken. I whimpered to the people still in the huddle, holding arms and chanting, "Guys, something is not right. I need some help." They looked at me with disgust as I wasn't part of their tribe. I stumbled my way up to the door and staggered my way around to the back of the house. I fell to my knees and finally purged myself of the leftover mushrooms in my stomach. I then rolled on the grass, and as the grass grew around my head, I lay there. I just lay there. It was a lovely summer night, and the grass was cool on my face, holding me like an old friend. I felt myself coming back to reality. It took some time, but then a crowd came and checked on me. What was amazing was that I felt totally sober, and the psychedelic effects were all gone. A few people helped me to my feet, and the friend of a friend took me to his house to sleep off the rest of the lingering mushroom trip.

In hindsight, those experiences taught me more than any lecture or warning ever could. Curiosity and impatience can be dangerous when combined with poor judgment. I was lucky to walk away with a few good stories instead of lifelong consequences. The truth is, every choice has a price, and sometimes we do not realize how high that price can be until we are already paying it. Life has a way of teaching lessons that stick, and some of mine just happened to come wrapped in bad decisions and good luck. I learned that wisdom usually arrives after the mistake, not before it.

REFLECTION:

Looking back, I can see that many of the lessons that shaped me came from choices I made, even though I knew they were not the smartest. I ignored warnings, pushed limits, and convinced myself that the rules somehow didn't apply. Every time I played one of those games, life made sure I earned the prize for my effort. The consequences were often hard, but they were honest, and honesty has a way of forcing growth. The older I get, the more I realize that life always keeps score, and every decision adds something to the tally. Some lessons came with scars, but those scars remind me that I am still here, still learning, and still capable of doing better. Growth doesn't come from pretending to be perfect; it comes from owning the mess and deciding not to repeat it.

READER'S REFLECTION:

1. What patterns or choices keep leading you to the same kind of pain or disappointment?
2. When have you ignored your own intuition and paid the price for it later?
3. How do you recognize when a situation or person isn't worth the cost anymore?
4. What lessons have been repeated in your life until you finally decided to change?
5. What would it look like to stop participating in things that don't serve your peace or progress?

The Importance of Saying No

I know what it feels like to be so overwhelmed that nothing I do seems to make a difference. I lived most of my life as a people pleaser. Growing up without validation shaped me into someone who tried to earn approval anywhere I could find it. It is the mind's way of overcompensating for what it missed, trying to make sure that old wounds never get reopened. I went out of my way for others far more than I ever did for myself. That included work. Some people call it brown-nosing, but for me, it was about purpose. When someone trusted me with more work than anyone else, it felt like I mattered. I did not realize how deep that pattern went until a few years ago. When I finally stopped and paid attention, I noticed it happened during a period of high stress. I was not sleeping. I was always worried about the future. I kept putting everyone else's needs above my own. When life feels like it is collapsing in on itself, that is the time to step back and evaluate what truly needs to change.

Learning to say no changed everything for me. We all have limits. We all have the same twenty-four hours in a day, and some days feel chaotic enough that if breathing were not automatic, I would forget to do it. Life throws curveballs without warning, and we adjust because we have no choice. I used to be like Jim Carrey in *Yes Man*. Every request, every task, every favor, I was in. It is exhausting to live without any "me time". Some people have families, children, demanding jobs, or social circles that expect constant presence. There are endless reasons we become overwhelmed, but knowing where the line is matters.

FOMO is real. Whether it is hanging out with friends or attempting to be at every meeting at work, the fear of missing something grabs hold. It is human instinct to worry that something meaningful will happen and we will not be there. I learned quickly that saying no requires intention. If I tell someone off, especially a boss, there will be consequences. Saying no is not about being reckless. It is about being deliberate in how I communicate boundaries.

In 2024, I had an inside salesperson who refused to participate in pricing a large variety of units we were preparing to manufacture. His excuse was always the same. "I don't understand the ERP system." He was scheduled to receive a commission on the sales, but only after production had started. He did not want to invest time in anything that did not pay him immediately. His priority was himself. Meanwhile, I was involved in every single aspect of this project, including physically assembling the product. As production increased, I needed to offload responsibilities, but I kept saying yes because I wanted the project to succeed.

Sales did nothing yet would receive commission on every unit. That bothered me. I finally called him and explained that I no longer had the availability to continue handling pricing, which was shared between inside and outside sales. He admitted he did not have time to learn the system. I told him I understood, but I did not have the time or resources either. I suggested we bring in the VP of Sales and the VP of Operations on a call to help determine who could assist us with pricing. Silence. A long one. Then suddenly, he said, "I can help you. Let's meet in the morning so I can learn how you're doing this."

That was the moment the dynamic shifted. I stopped being taken advantage of. He knew that if executives got involved, he would end up doing the work anyway. I did not have to accuse him of slacking or call him a worthless prick, even though I wanted to. I made it clear that the current setup was not sustainable. Yes, it was a bit of psychology. Not dark psychology, but enough of a strategic nudge to force accountability. For the first time, I said no.

Another time, at this same company, I realized I could no longer stay in the division I worked in. I was burned out, unhappy, and sank deeper into exhaustion. I spoke with the higher-ups and told them I wanted out. I repeatedly asked for help, but I wouldn't get it. Every day, I fell further behind.

They finally offered help, but the drawn-out hiring process took forever. At this point and in this case, I knew I was done. When they asked me to stay and train my replacement, I said no. I could not justify stepping up for them when they never stepped up for me. I put in my notice. I always recommend having another job lined up, but I was drained from working sixty-five to seventy hours a week with no end in sight. People like to say "that's what you signed up for," but they are not the ones carrying the load.

In my final two weeks, I refused to work weekends and capped my days at ten hours. My stress level dropped from a ten to a four. I stopped killing myself to keep up and left the backlog for the next guy. He had been trying to sabotage me anyway. I wished him the best. May he recover from the strain of constantly patting himself on the back. When I finally said no and walked away, I felt human again.

Saying no changed my life. I stopped running myself into the ground trying to please everyone else. I started protecting my time, energy, and sanity. At first, it felt uncomfortable, almost wrong, but I realized something important. Most people will take as much as they can get until a boundary is set. Once I set them, my sleep improved, my stress decreased, and I actually enjoyed life again. Saying no is not rude or selfish. It is self-respect. It is reclaiming my peace. The moment I started saying no, I took back control of my life.

REFLECTION:

I always thought saying yes was the only way to prove my worth. I said yes to opportunities, to people, and to responsibilities that often drained me. I didn't realize how much of myself I was giving away until I had nothing left. The more I tried to please everyone around me, the more I lost sight of who I was. It took a long time to understand that saying no wasn't selfish. It is survival. It's choosing to protect my energy rather than hand it out to everyone who asks for it. When I started saying no, I felt guilt at first, but then I noticed the space it created. That space allowed me to breathe, to think, and to give more intentionally. Every time I said no to something that didn't align with me, I was quietly saying yes to the things that did. Learning to

84

say no became one of the most freeing decisions of my life. It taught me that peace didn't come from doing everything for everyone, but came from finally doing what's right for me.

READER'S REFLECTION:

1. When was the last time you said yes to something that drained you instead of filled you?
2. What fears or guilt come up for you when you think about saying no?
3. How does setting boundaries protect not just your time, but your energy and self-worth?
4. Who or what in your life deserves a confident no, so you can say yes to what really matters?
5. How might your relationships change if you started saying no from a place of self-respect instead of avoidance?

Finding Your Tribe

W e all need to feel loved and like we belong. It is one of the five basic human needs described by Abraham Maslow. Human beings are social creatures who require love, connection, and acceptance. It is a basic need that most of us take for granted until it is missing. The older I get, the less I care about quantity and the more I care about quality. A person can be surrounded by hundreds of people and still feel completely alone. Another person may have only one or two people they cannot live without. Some people stay close to their families. Others build community through church, recovery groups, gaming communities, online circles, and so on. Wherever it comes from, real belonging feels like home. We are the only ones who truly know what we need, and making sure we keep the right kind of company matters.

I cannot emphasize this enough. Being around the right crowd determines the direction of my life. Most of us have certain people we call to vent, confide in, or break down with. When I was desperate for friends, I learned the hard way that people in addiction often pull others into their same vacuum. Even when I said I did not want to do something, they kept pushing and pressuring me until I felt worn down. It was never about my interests. It was about theirs. They wanted someone sitting in the gutter next to them so they did not feel alone. At the time, I mistook that for connection. It was a misery recruiting company. I tried to be around people who were stuck in that loop without falling back into it, and I realized it is impossible.

Anyone who has ever stepped away from a partying crowd knows exactly what I mean. When sober alternatives are offered, the group rejects anything that does not involve drinking. That is especially true in the Midwest, where drinking culture runs deep and winters are long and isolating. People itch to get together, and the tavern becomes the default meeting place. Once I became the sober person in the group, everything changed. Their habits, their noise, their chaos grated on me. That was not my tribe.

Mental health plays a massive role in who we gravitate toward. Poor mental health impacts physical health, and vice versa. It is the chicken-or-the-egg scenario. Many of us go through periods where everything feels off. It becomes a recurring cycle. Sometimes it has everything to do with who we spend time with. I discovered I had been part of the toxicity, too. I was not helping anyone escape the loop because I was stuck in it myself. When I finally got out, the same people who dragged me back in would not follow. I stopped beating myself up for leaving. I accepted that I no longer belonged in that tribe. I grew. They didn't, or maybe they eventually did, but I stopped making the effort to reconnect.

I am still searching for my tribe, the people who make me better. The ones who push me out of my comfort zone. The ones who want to build something meaningful and are willing to put in the effort. Anyone else on the same path knows how it feels. It is okay to be still searching. The right people will come about in due time. They offer the mind a place to go when we need space from our own minds. They will show up, and I will do the same. Things should never be one-sided. I had a friend who only called when he needed something. I reached out often, and he always responded with "I'm busy." Yet whenever he asked for something, I dropped everything. After a while, I stopped responding. He eventually stopped trying and removed me from his social media accounts. At some point, taking advantage crosses a line that cannot be ignored.

It is easier to walk away from toxic friends. It is far harder with family. For my own mental health, I had to set boundaries, even when it felt uncomfortable. It is critical to protect the inner circle. I remind myself often that I deserve relationships that support my life rather than drain it. If the right people have not shown up yet, it is not the end of the story. They are out there. Sometimes we have to start the conversation. Sometimes timing is off.

Sometimes life paths are different. The search continues, and that is okay.

When I stopped chasing the wrong people, I finally started finding the right ones. It took honesty and brutal self-reflection to admit that I was part of the problem for a long time. Once I made peace with that, my life became quieter and better. The noise faded. The chaos disappeared. The people who remained were the ones who truly cared. Finding a tribe is not about having a crowd. It is about finding a circle that helps me grow and keeps me grounded. When people bring out the best in me, I hold on to them. That is when belonging feels real.

REFLECTION:

I thought independence meant strength, and that needing people made me weak. Over time, I learned that life feels heavier when it is walked alone. The people around me have the power to lift me up or pull me under, and I had to learn to tell the difference. Finding my tribe has been about discovering the ones who see me for who I am, flaws and all, and still choose to stay. The ones who push me to grow, even when it is uncomfortable, and remind me that I am not alone when life feels like too much. I have lost people I thought would be in my life forever, and I have gained others I never expected to find. The right people make the weight of life easier to bear. They stand beside me in silence when words are not enough and celebrate my wins as if they were their own. Finding my tribe has taught me that belonging is not about fitting in. It is about finding peace with who I am while standing beside those who do the same.

READER'S REFLECTION:

1. Who in your life truly sees and accepts you for who you are?
2. How do you know when someone is part of your "tribe" versus just part of your circle?
3. What qualities do you value most in genuine connection and friendship?
4. Have you ever outgrown people you once felt close to, and how did you

handle that shift?

5. What steps can you take to surround yourself with people who encourage your growth and authenticity?

Practicing Gratitude

In the face of everything life throws my way, I have learned how important it is to express gratitude. It is easy to forget what matters most or to overlook what I already have. Being grateful is a state of mind, and gratitude is what it feels like when I truly live in that awareness. I first learned this in a leadership class through work when the instructor suggested taking a minute each morning to reflect on what I was thankful for. It sounded simple, but it made a real difference. I had been so focused on what I didn't have that I rarely stopped to appreciate what was already positive in my life.

I began each morning by quietly acknowledging the things that mattered most to me: my wife, my parents, my family, and the home we built with our own blood, sweat, and tears. I thought about the coworkers and bosses who helped me grow, and even the difficult ones who taught me how not to act. I realized that people are either blessings or lessons, and both have value. I'm also grateful for anyone who has taken the time to read my words and walk through these stories with me. Some of them have been hard to tell, but I hope they've made someone laugh, feel seen, or find a lesson that helps them through their own life.

One of the most challenging parts of my journey has been learning how to show gratitude to myself. I spent years chasing validation from others and rarely stopped to recognize my own progress. When I finally did, I realized there was a lot to be proud of. I accomplished things that once felt impossible, even when I didn't see them that way at the time. I remind myself that I already won the first race I ever ran, and I beat every other possibility just to be here. That's something worth honoring.

Gratitude doesn't have to come from grand moments. It's often in the most minor things, like making a meal for my family. It takes effort to plan, shop, prepare, serve, and clean up, and those moments remind me what it means to care for the people I love. I've learned to slow down and appreciate being together, whether it is cooking, talking, or just being in their company. I wasn't raised to stop and savor moments like that. I was always focused on the next task, the next goal, the next deadline. School and work trained that constant forward motion into me. But now, I make it a point to pause, take a deep breath, and think about what truly matters in my life.

When I dwell on mistakes, I try to give myself some amnesty. I've made plenty of them, but each one taught me something valuable. I used to beat myself up for every misstep, but I've realized that being human is reason enough to forgive myself. I do what I can to make amends when possible, and when I can't, I remind myself that some things just aren't meant to be. There is always something new to discover, something or someone else to appreciate, even when life feels uncertain.

Helping Bonnie tell her story is something I am deeply grateful for. Her courage gives others hope, and I am proud of her for finding her voice. There are times I wish she had been able to leave her situation sooner, but then I remind myself that everything unfolded the way it was supposed to. If she had left earlier, maybe our paths never would have crossed. She could have been hurt or worse, and that thought alone makes me thankful that life worked out as it did. I didn't want to break her story into smaller parts because it deserved to be told as one whole, uninterrupted truth. It is a story of pain and resilience, and I am forever grateful she is part of my life.

Gratitude changed how I see the world. It doesn't erase pain or struggle, but it shifts my focus toward what is still good and worth holding on to. I remind myself every day that even in the most challenging moments, there is always something to be thankful for. Some days, it is as simple as a warm meal or a quiet night at home. Other days, it's the people who refused to give up on me, even when I was ready to give up on myself. The more I've learned to appreciate the simple things, the fuller and lighter life has become.

Gratitude isn't about what I've lost. It's about recognizing what I still have and realizing how much of it truly matters. I wake up and say what I am grateful for before I get up and start my day, getting my mind right to deal with the day ahead.

REFLECTION:

Gratitude has become more than just saying thank you for me; it is a way of seeing the world differently. I used to focus so much on what I didn't have that I rarely noticed what was already right in front of me. Over time, I learned that gratitude doesn't erase struggle or pain, but it changes how I carry those feelings. When I make a point of recognizing what is still good, the weight of everything else becomes easier to bear. I remind myself that even on the worst days, there is always something to appreciate, like a quiet morning, a kind word, a meal shared, or simply the fact that I woke up to see another day. Gratitude grounds me in the present. It keeps me from drifting too far into regret about the past or anxiety about the future. It reminds me that life will always hold something worth valuing, even in the middle of the chaos. The more I practice it, the more I notice how peace starts to replace worry, and appreciation starts to outweigh anger or fear. Gratitude doesn't require everything to be perfect; it just asks that I pay attention to what is still good.

READER'S REFLECTION:

1. When was the last time you slowed down and truly felt grateful for something small?
2. How does gratitude change the way you see your challenges or hardships?
3. Who in your life deserves a thank-you that you haven't said out loud yet?
4. What daily moments do you often overlook that could become reminders of appreciation?
5. How could gratitude become a regular mindset instead of an occasional

feeling?

Social Media Has Its Strengths and Weaknesses

Having all the information in the world at our fingertips has been a benefit and a curse. Every time someone posts something, internet trolls and keyboard warriors emerge from their mother's basement to try to provoke a response. It adds a unique twist to self-doubt. I have had countless attacks on my person or thoughts by people stating negative or mean things. I have also been guilty of reciprocating in that way, as the items posted are not debates; they are little frustrating moments where someone chose to display negativity, and I snapped and attacked their character. It is really easy to say something that you will regret. They are all "tough guys or gals" from behind a keyboard, but would never say things to your face. Don't even waste your time with those bottom-feeders. They are so miserable with their life that they must belittle someone to make themselves feel better or laugh at you. It is a sad world when someone takes a statement or a vulnerable moment and twists it to try to elicit a reaction from others. I increasingly see that people are becoming more alienated, alone, and less capable of rational communication. We spend more time glued to our screens than looking each other in the eye. Society is hooked on scrolling, peering, swiping, and reacting to everyone's posts and reels. The good, the bad; we, as a society, are addicted. It adds to everyone's FOMO.

The internet isn't all bad. I actually met my wife online. I added her as a friend on Facebook and liked some of her photos without much thought. One day, I was browsing Facebook and saw a photo of her in a photoshoot, which featured a simple beaded headband and necklace, along with a pink bikini adorned with suede fringe. The style was loosely inspired by Native American attire, but to me it looked more like a sixties hippie outfit. The number of people offended by the outfit was remarkable. I stood up for her because there was nothing offensive, demeaning, or harmful depicted against Native Americans. They probably would be the same people who would wear a cheap Native American outfit and think nothing of it for Halloween. I know I am biased on this, but it is just that many of the examples of the abuse people feel. For her, it was simply part of rebuilding her self-confidence and pursuing her dream of modeling, because she had been unable to do so before. Having someone knock her already low confidence down even further was despicable. People are going through more than you know on the surface, and it's always best to try to be kind.

After that, we started chatting quite a bit and eventually went on a first date. One memory from that night that still makes us laugh: the around-the-world cheese platter. It had cheeses, meats, fruits, jams, breads, and crackers. Everything was really appetizing except for one thing. There was this goat cheese that tasted EXACTLY like a barn room floor. I grew up on a farm, so I know the barn smell, and this tasted like the cheese was sitting directly on stale hay and manure. I tried the bouquet of barn cheese and used my best poker face, saying, "You should try this." Now, this could have been one of the reasons the date failed, but she tried it. Her face puckered, and she immediately grabbed the napkin and spat it out. It was a gamble, but we both laughed and will never forget that. As I stated in an earlier chapter, our brains don't retain everyday occurrences. They hold onto the weird, the unexpected, and the memorable.

Had the date not gone as planned, we both would have gone on with our lives, and things probably would have been drastically different for each of us. The important thing is that we wanted to create a life together and both put in effort. We also both support each other's pursuits and are each other's greatest cheerleader. Sorry for the potential visual of me in a cheerleader outfit; maybe "supporter" is a better term. If two different people had that exact experience, one person might not have been happy, and the date could have ended badly. Even if that was the case, we cannot control other people's reactions; all we can do is control how we react if the date doesn't go well. It is what it is. We cannot force something to work. That includes a relationship that is failing if no mutual effort is made to improve it. We can put in effort, and it still fails; that might not be entirely on us. The other person really didn't want it to work and wanted it to be over. And while that hurts, it clears space for something healthier in the long run.

Social media will always have its strengths and weaknesses, and I have lived on both sides of it. I have seen how it can destroy someone's confidence in a single post, but I have also seen how it can change a life for the better. It connected me to my wife and gave us a chance to build something tangible out of a digital world that often feels fake. Over time, I learned to stop feeding into negativity and to focus on what mattered. I use it now to stay in touch with people who bring value, not drama. It took a long time to find that balance, but when we learn to use social media rather than letting it use us, it becomes a tool for growth rather than a weapon.

REFLECTION:

Social media has been both a gift and a curse in my life. It connects me to people I might never meet or rarely see otherwise, gives me a platform to share ideas, and allows me to stay informed in ways once impossible. But I have also seen how easily it can distort reality. I have caught myself comparing my life to carefully curated highlight reels and wondering why my everyday moments didn't seem as exciting or successful. It took time to realize that social media is not the whole picture; it's a reflection of what people choose to show. I've learned to be more intentional with how I use it, to set boundaries, and to step back when it starts to affect my peace of mind. The truth is that the likes, comments, and followers don't define who I am. They don't measure worth or happiness. When I take the time to unplug and be present in my real life by sharing a meal, taking a walk, laughing with someone I love, that is when I feel connected in a way no screen can match. Social media can be a tool for growth or a trap for insecurity, and that choice is entirely mine.

READER'S REFLECTION:

1. How often do you compare your real life to someone else's highlight reel online?

2. What emotions come up when you spend too much time scrolling — validation, envy, disconnection, or something else?

3. How could you use social media more intentionally, to connect, inspire, or learn, instead of to escape?

4. What boundaries might help you protect your mental and emotional space online?

5. When was the last time you disconnected completely and felt more present as a result?

Don't Overshare

It is imperative to stay mindful of what belongs in the public eye and what should remain private. I have friends on social media who constantly share personal problems and harmful content, and it only creates chaos. I learned that keeping public things public and private things private protects not only peace of mind but also relationships. It can be tempting to post something emotional to see who shows support, but that approach usually causes more harm than good. It drags others into situations they never asked to be part of and often forces those close to explain or defend things they had nothing to do with. I have been in that position before, and it is exhausting. It becomes a constant reminder of someone else's turmoil, replayed for an audience that never asked to see it. People already carry their own struggles. Adding more noise only strains connections that might otherwise be supportive.

Negativity breeds more of the same. Being around a person who constantly complains or spreads negativity is emotionally draining. I avoid that energy whenever possible. Sometimes that even meant confronting it directly. I once had to tell someone close to me that the constant stream of negativity was becoming too much. I explained that it was affecting my mental health and that I could not keep absorbing that energy every day. It was not an easy conversation, but it was necessary. In that moment, I realized that honesty, when expressed calmly, can be a powerful form of self-care. Not everyone will take it well, and that is okay. What matters is drawing the line before being pulled under by someone else's storm.

Of course, everyone needs to vent from time to time. A good rant can even be healthy. But too much of it becomes toxic, especially when it consumes every conversation. I started taking mental notes about the people I spent the most time with and how I felt after being around them. Some left me feeling inspired or lighthearted, while others left me feeling completely drained. The difference became impossible to ignore. I learned to distance myself from the people who only brought problems and to spend more time with those who brought peace.

In today's world, it feels like everyone is performing for an audience, even when they do not realize it. Every thought, photo, and reaction is broadcast, and the line between personal and public life blurs. I am guilty of it too. There were times I shared things that should have stayed private, thinking I was being open or honest, but it only led to regret. The truth is that once something is shared, it is no longer under your control. Someone can screenshot it, share it, twist it, or bring it up years later when it no longer reflects who you are. The internet does not forget. I have seen friendships and jobs ruined over a single post made in anger or pain. It taught me that protecting my peace sometimes means safeguarding my ability to be silent.

Not every emotion deserves an audience, and not every thought needs validation. I used to think vulnerability meant sharing everything, but I eventually learned that real vulnerability is about knowing when to share and with whom. There is power in privacy. It allows space to process, to heal, and to grow without external noise or judgment. The people who genuinely care do not need a post to know what is happening. They reach out because they already see or feel it. I have learned to share my joy, my lessons, and my growth, but to keep the storms private until I am ready to talk about them from a place of peace, not pain.

Oversharing can feel like relief in the moment, but it often creates long-term regret. There is a reason peace feels quiet. I choose to keep certain parts of my life off social media and within a small circle that I trust. The less I feed the public machine, the more grounded I feel. There is a freedom in not needing to perform, in not having to explain, and in not giving everyone access to every emotion. The more I protected my private life, the stronger and calmer I became. It is not about hiding who I am; it is about valuing who

I am enough to protect it.

Privacy is not isolation; it is preservation. The people who genuinely care are the ones who physically check in, not the ones who comment. Protecting my peace became more critical than public validation. Sharing joy, good news, and positivity are still essential, but personal storms belong in safe, trusted circles. The less energy I give to drama, the more I have left for the things that truly matter.

REFLECTION:

I have learned the hard way that once something is shared publicly, it is no longer fully mine. Whether it is a post, a story, or even a conversation that slips into the wrong hands, it can take on a life of its own. I have seen words twisted, intentions misread, and moments of vulnerability turned into gossip. There were times I shared too much, hoping for connection or understanding, only to regret it later when I realized how exposed it made me feel. Over time, I learned that protecting my privacy is not about secrecy; it is about self-respect. My story deserves to be told in the right way, at the right time, and to the right people. I no longer feel obligated to share every detail of my life to prove authenticity. Vulnerability has power, but it is strongest when guided by wisdom. Keeping certain parts of my life private has given me peace, and that peace is worth more than public attention.

READER'S REFLECTION:

1. Before you share something personal, do you ever ask yourself why and who it's really for?
2. What parts of your life feel sacred enough to keep private?
3. How has oversharing or vulnerability in the wrong space ever left you feeling exposed or misunderstood?
4. How can you tell the difference between sharing for connection and sharing for validation?
5. What would it mean to you to protect your peace, even if it means keeping

some stories just for yourself?

Honesty Might Lead to Ridicule

W hy in the hell would I share some of the events that happened to me and embarrass myself? I do it so others might learn something without having to go through the same pain. Every story I tell comes from a moment that was far from ordinary, one that burned itself into memory. When I look back, I can see each one as either a life lesson or a reason to beat myself up, depending on the lens I choose. That is the strange gift of experience; it can be both a blessing and a bane, depending on how it is viewed. I have learned that by being honest and open about my past, I will attract both compassion and ridicule. That balance is simply part of being human.

We are all conditioned to look down on others. Maybe it starts in childhood, watching a classmate get sent to the corner or seeing someone get mocked for a mistake while the rest of the room laughs. I remember moments like that, times when I felt empathy while others found entertainment. That early conditioning follows us into adulthood. The human condition itself is a strange paradox; we crave connection, yet we often judge one another harshly. Philosophers and writers have debated for centuries about what drives us: meaning, morality, suffering, knowledge, love, and the search for happiness. I am no philosopher, but I have lived enough to know that being human means being both flawed and capable of redemption.

There is an old proverb: *People in glass houses should not throw stones*. That saying has aged well. Everyone has something they do not want seen or compared, and yet those people still seem eager to cast judgment. Reactions to honesty are shaped by countless factors such as personal experience, upbringing, religion, trauma, culture, politics, or fear of being different. The list never ends. I am not here to argue what is right or wrong, and I do not care to. People will always believe what they believe. I have chosen to focus on empathy rather than cynicism. The world has enough negativity without me adding more. I can accept criticism when it is constructive, but cruelty for the sake of cruelty says more about the person delivering it than the one receiving it.

I have been on the receiving end of ridicule, both online and in person. I have dealt with keyboard warriors, people who feel brave behind a screen and free to tear others apart. Before social media, gossip used to happen behind closed doors. Now it is broadcast for anyone to see, replayed endlessly, and impossible to take back. I live by one principle: what people say about me is none of my business. Some days, that is easier said than done, but holding on to that mindset has saved me more peace than any argument ever could.

Everyone experiences peaks and valleys in life. The lows test character, while the highs remind us of why we keep going. When I fall, I try to rise quickly and forgive myself faster. Life is a constant series of blank canvases. Sometimes the painting turns out beautifully, and other times it needs to be painted over. When I fail, I allow myself to feel it, learn from it, and then move forward. Being present is far more productive than reliving past mistakes. The past cannot be changed, but the future is still being written.

Inner peace is fragile, and honesty can either strengthen or shatter it depending on where it is placed. I have learned to be careful about who earns access to the personal parts of my life. Trust is currency, and not everyone deserves the same level of investment. I connect more easily with people who share openly about their own struggles. It helps me feel seen, but it can also backfire if I share too much too soon. Honesty is freeing, but it can become ammunition in the wrong hands.

Even as I write these words, there is a quiet voice in the back of my head anticipating judgment. But that voice no longer stops me. I know some will read my truth and roll their eyes, mock it, or dismiss it. Others will see themselves in it and feel a little less alone. That is the trade-off of transparency. The world may judge, but honesty connects us in ways that pretending never could.

Honesty has always made me vulnerable, but it has also made me free. The more open I became about who I am, the more I attracted people who belong in my life and lost the ones who never did. Not everyone deserves my whole story, and that is okay. The goal is not perfection or approval; it is authenticity. People will always have opinions, but those opinions cannot define me unless I allow them to. I would rather be ridiculed for being real than praised for being fake.

REFLECTION:

Being honest has not always come easy for me, and it certainly has not always been rewarded. There have been times when speaking the truth made me a target for ridicule, judgment, or even rejection. Yet, I have learned that the discomfort of honesty is far less painful than the burden of pretending. Each time I chose to tell the truth, I felt a small piece of weight lift off my shoulders, even if it came with criticism or misunderstanding. Being open about my life has cost me at times, but it has also set me free. The more I have embraced honesty, the less I care about seeking approval from those who only value appearances. It took me years to realize that honesty is not about being perfect or seeking validation; it is about living in alignment with who I really am. Some people have mocked or criticized me for being open, but those voices no longer matter. What matters is that I can look in the mirror and know I am being real. Honesty has cleared away so many illusions, both in how I see others and in how I see myself. It has brought the right people together and allowed me to grow without the constant fear of exposure. The cost of honesty can be steep, but the cost of hiding is far greater, and I would rather stand in my truth than live behind a mask.

READER'S REFLECTION:

1. When have you told the truth and been judged or misunderstood because of it?
2. What fears come up when you think about being fully honest about your experiences or emotions?
3. How do you balance being authentic with protecting your peace?
4. Who in your life makes it safe for you to speak your truth without fear of ridicule?
5. What would it look like to keep being honest even if others don't always understand you?

Communication Is Key

I never really had anyone around when I was a child to help me develop my communication skills. Growing up without someone to talk to or play with made it difficult to trust others or express what I felt. It took years to realize how much that silence shaped me. Being an only child from a broken home can leave you at a disadvantage because there is rarely anyone who goes out of their way to be there for you. I also avoided letting people in, afraid of being hurt again. That is no way to live. It took a long time to feel comfortable trusting myself and others when communicating, and even now, I still work at it.

There are four main parts of communication that I had to learn from scratch: awareness, listening, speaking, and dialogue. They are the building blocks of every interaction. Some people naturally talk and share everything about their lives, while others remain vaults that never open. I fell somewhere in between, trying to find balance. Communication is not just about talking; it is also about understanding the timing, tone, and who is saying what to whom.

Awareness comes first. Some people call it reading the room. There are times and places to say certain things, and there are moments when silence is the wiser choice. I still think back to a situation in a hotel years ago when I made an unintentional remark that was offensive to that specific group. It taught me a valuable lesson about awareness. The same principle applies in every setting, especially at work. I once had to reprimand an employee for poor behavior and safety issues. After being corrected, that same person asked for more responsibility. It was almost surreal to hear. Awareness means recognizing when the moment is not right and adjusting accordingly.

Sensitivity matters, too. If someone has experienced a loss, a trauma, or anything deeply personal, awareness helps prevent careless words from adding to their pain. People do not always share what they have been through, so I approach conversations with respect for what I may not know. Not everyone will tell you when something hurts them, but it shows quickly enough through body language or withdrawal. It is easy to overlook those signs, but awareness keeps me grounded in empathy.

The following piece is active listening. There is an old saying about having two ears and one mouth, so we can listen twice as much as we speak. I used to be terrible at that. While someone was talking, my mind was already jumping ahead to what I would say next. I often interrupted or tried to slip in jokes to get a laugh, looking for validation rather than connection. That kind of listening is just noise waiting for its turn to talk. Genuine listening takes effort, focus, and humility.

Listening is not only physical but also nonverbal. It means putting down the phone, turning off distractions, and giving the person across from me full attention. Few things are more discouraging than opening up about something important only to realize the other person is half-listening while checking messages. When I listen now, I try to make eye contact and read the other person's cues. Communication is as much about what is not said as what is spoken.

Speaking comes next, and it carries weight. Words can heal or destroy depending on how they are used. I communicate with intention and remain calm, even when emotions run high. Raising my voice never solved anything. When conversations get heated, people often bring up unrelated issues just to win an argument. I have done that before, and it never ends well. Staying on topic and addressing one problem at a time prevents unnecessary damage. Speaking clearly means respecting both myself and the person I am talking with.

Dialogue is the back-and-forth, the exchange that keeps a conversation alive. I like to think of it like tennis: one side serves, the other responds, and the rhythm continues. Sometimes the points are quick, and some drag on. Healthy dialogue allows ideas, feelings, and perspectives to move freely, even when opinions differ. Not every conversation needs agreement, but every conversation should aim for understanding.

Looking back on the arguments and conversations I have had, there is always something I could have done differently. I cannot control how others react, but I can control my words, my tone, and my willingness to listen. That awareness alone makes a difference. Walking away from a conversation knowing I handled myself with patience and honesty feels better than winning an argument I will regret later.

Learning to communicate changed how I connect with people and how I see myself. For many years, I avoided difficult discussions and spoke before truly listening. When I finally slowed down and started paying attention, I realized communication is not just about words; it is about connection. The ability to understand before responding can save relationships, prevent pain, and build trust. The more I practiced, the more peace I found in every part of my life. Speaking clearly and listening fully has taught me that every conversation, no matter how small, is a chance to learn something new about myself and the person in front of me.

REFLECTION:

I have learned that every relationship in my life, whether personal or professional, rises or falls based on how well I communicate. When I fail to express what I feel or avoid the conversations I need to have, things always get worse. Misunderstandings grow, assumptions fill the gaps, and trust starts to fade. Communication is not just about speaking my mind; it is about listening with intent, understanding what the other person is really trying to say, and responding with honesty and respect. I have learned that holding back feelings to keep the peace only creates deeper tension later. The times I have been most honest, even when it was uncomfortable, have been the moments that built the strongest connections in my life. Communication is not always easy, but it is always worth it. When I speak clearly, listen fully, and stay grounded in empathy, I find that walls begin to fall and real trust begins to form.

READER'S REFLECTION:

1. When was the last time a lack of communication created unnecessary tension or misunderstanding?
2. How do you tend to communicate when emotions are high, with openness or defensiveness?
3. What relationships in your life would improve if you listened to understand instead of to respond?
4. How can you express your needs more clearly without fear of conflict or rejection?
5. What does honest, respectful communication look like for you at your best?

Relationships Are Hard Work

As you well know, relationships are hard work, and I am preaching to the choir. Even though most people already understand this, I want to walk through a few lessons I have learned and share a story about what not to do. There are times when I have taken my significant other for granted. It is easy to become comfortable with the things they do and stop noticing the effort they put in. That comfort can quietly turn into resentment when something that once felt like a gesture becomes an expectation. I spend all day at work pushing projects forward, solving problems, and keeping things running, but when I get home, the same amount of work still waits for me in a different form. The problem is that there are fewer hours to do it in. Finding a balance between priorities and what can wait is essential. Everyone has their own set of needs, but I have learned that understanding my partner's needs is just as crucial as understanding my own.

In traditional relationships, and speaking only from my experience, men often put in more effort at the beginning. That early drive to impress and connect tends to fade over time, but it shouldn't. The same energy that starts a relationship is the same energy that keeps it alive. Both people have to stay invested. When only one person carries the weight, that imbalance turns into frustration, and that's where good relationships start to die. I have been guilty of not noticing when that balance started to shift. Nobody deserves to feel unappreciated. The moment effort stops being mutual, resentment begins to grow in the cracks that communication once filled.

When that happens, I always ask myself what comes next. Do I walk away and burn the ships so there's no turning back? If I were immature, maybe.

But being civil and respectful, even in conflict, says a lot about my character. I can't control how someone else reacts, only how I do. When I've wanted to make things work, I've learned that wanting change and creating it are two very different things. Real progress takes work from both sides. That means identifying the root of the problem, even when it hurts. Talking honestly, without yelling, blaming, or letting ego take over, is the only way forward. Throwing flaws back and forth doesn't solve anything. The conversation might not always end ideally, but staying engaged and working on the issues is what keeps things from breaking completely.

I remember a relationship I thought would last forever. I ignored the red flags as things started to fall apart. When she graduated from school, she wanted to move back to her family in a big city. I didn't mind visiting them, but I had no interest in living there. I kept hoping she would change her mind, but she had already chosen the life she wanted. I tried to hold things together, but she was already slipping away. It hurt deeply because she had been the reason I went back to school and started bettering myself. When she left, it felt like my world stopped spinning. I carried that pain for a long time, convinced I had failed. I couldn't eat, couldn't sleep, and kept replaying conversations in my head, trying to figure out what I could have done differently. Eventually, I started focusing on myself again, and slowly, I began to heal. Time doesn't erase pain, but it gives perspective. Every wound scabs over differently, but eventually, it stops bleeding. That breakup forced me to rebuild myself piece by piece and taught me that sometimes love ends not because someone stops caring, but because they start growing in different directions.

This next story is about a former friend who had a volatile and destructive relationship. He started dating someone I had known from school years earlier. We were only acquaintances, and I didn't know much about her. At first, it seemed harmless enough. They started dating, and I thought it was great that he had found someone. But soon after, she was being evicted from her apartment and needed a place to stay. He wanted to help and asked her to move in with him. It was after only three weeks of dating. That was the beginning of the chaos. Three weeks is not enough time to truly know someone.

I have always believed that living with someone before marriage can be a good idea because it shows how well you actually get along day to day. But moving in together out of financial desperation is not the same thing. After marriage, separation becomes more complicated, especially when shared assets, children, or pets are involved. I have seen how hard it can be when two people realize too late that their standards of living or values do not align. Moving in can work under the right circumstances, but only after real time has passed and trust is built. Anyone can behave for a few weeks. In this case, he was behind on his bills and needed help paying them. She was facing eviction. That combination of fear and convenience created the perfect storm. Financial need is never a good reason to move someone in.

A few more weeks passed, and I invited them over. She brought her two kids, and everything seemed fine on the surface. She scolded her son once, but it was nothing alarming. He seemed genuinely happy at that point, and I was glad to see it. That did not last long. Around their three-month mark, he called me late at night in a panic. She had started screaming and throwing things, and he locked himself in a room to get away. She grabbed a hammer, smashed the doorknob off, and broke through the door. His voice was shaking when he called. I could hear her screaming in the background. It was chaos. When he hung up, I was left sitting there, staring at my phone, not knowing what to do. Later, he said she had finally calmed down and gone to bed. I told him to come to my place if it ever happened again.

The next day, it did. She started screaming again and hitting him. He came over, and when I saw him, I could tell he was broken down. He said it was happening almost every day. He even told me that she once smelled his underwear because she thought he was cheating. That was how far it had gone. Who does that? It was beyond jealousy. It was an obsession. He could not even form sentences properly anymore. At first, I thought it was stress. Later, I learned there was more to it.

I told him he needed to go to the police. He did, but they told him there was not much they could do because they were living together, and technically, it was her home. A week later, I got another call. He said she had grabbed a knife, and he was locked in the bathroom. I told him to leave immediately and come to my house. When he showed up, he had a mark on his eye. He called the police again to report it. Later that night, one of her friends grew worried because she wasn't responding to messages. The police did a welfare check, and somehow, he ended up being arrested for domestic disturbance. She had given herself bruises and marks, something she later admitted to her friend, who told me. I bailed him out, but he had to stay away for twenty-four hours. He stayed with another friend that time. I was not willing to have that kind of shit-show in my home.

About a week later, I got another photo from him while I was at work. His head was bleeding. She had hit him with her purse, which had a large metal brooch attached to it, and split his scalp open. He went to the hospital, and she was arrested and charged with domestic violence with intent to harm. She was held for 72 hours, posted bond, and immediately violated the no-contact order. Within a day, she was back harassing him. She began messaging me on social media. We were still connected online, and she started sending long rants accusing him of using meth and saying anything about everything. It became too much, and I blocked her.

Another week passed, and I got yet another call. This time, she had locked herself in the bathroom with a knife, threatening to kill herself. He told me she was in what he called sundown sickness, a term he used for meth withdrawal, when people become paranoid and violent. I told him to get out of the house. He showed up at my place again, this time with a black eye. She had texted him saying she was taking his car, and he told her not to because the control arm on the front end was bad. She took it anyway and went to a drug dealer's house. He had a GPS tracker on the vehicle, so he knew exactly where she was. He went to the police, and she was picked up again for another domestic dispute. He did not press charges for the stolen car, but a restraining order was filed against her.

She was not supposed to go near him, but she stayed with a friend and stole that friend's car to drive back to his house. I could not believe it when he told me. She showed up again, and instead of calling the police, he let her in. Predictably, another fight broke out, and he called the cops. That time, she was finally facing felony charges.

Eventually, she moved out, and his case was dropped after evidence proved she was the aggressor. He lost the house not long after because of the damage and unpaid rent. He moved about an hour away, trying to start fresh. For a brief moment, I thought maybe he was finally free. Then came another call. His tone was different, fast, frantic, and paranoid. He said something about passing a test and people trying to set him up. He rambled about a cult she used to be part of and how they were following him. His thoughts jumped all over the place. That was when he admitted he had been using meth regularly, while she was an occasional user. I was not sure what being an occasional user even meant. To make it worse, he said he was still seeing her again. That was it for me. I was done.

Cutting him off was one of the hardest things I have ever done, but I had to. That kind of madness will swallow you whole if you let it. It is like standing near a black hole. You get too close, and it pulls you in. It made me sad to know how far he had fallen, but he did not see his drug use as a problem. I did. Until he hit rock bottom and decided to climb out, there was nothing I could do. I learned that sometimes I have to love people from a distance for my own sanity and safety.

That whole ordeal taught me how destructive codependency can be. It is human nature to want to help, but when I am constantly rescuing someone who does not want to be saved, I end up drowning right alongside them. People caught in addiction live in survival mode, doing whatever it takes to feed the need. It is not their fault. The drugs hijack their mind and control their choices, but they have to choose to fight back. I cannot want them to recover more than they want to.

Real love is not about saving someone or fixing them. It is about standing beside a person who also wants to grow and do the work. A relationship should not drain someone's energy or make them question their worth. It should bring out the best parts of who we are. Sometimes walking away is the hardest choice, but it is also the most loving thing we can do for ourselves. When both people are willing to put in effort, communicate honestly, and face their flaws, things can work. When only one person tries, survival takes over and love disappears. I would rather be alone and at peace than stay in a relationship built on chaos and false hope.

REFLECTION:

I have learned that love is both work and wisdom. It demands effort, patience, and sacrifice, but it also requires the courage to recognize when effort becomes survival. For years, I believed that fighting for a relationship showed loyalty, but I eventually learned that love without balance can turn into exhaustion. Healthy relationships are built through communication, mutual respect, and the willingness to grow together, not by saving someone who refuses to save themselves. I have watched people destroy each other while calling it love, and I have felt the pull to fix what was never mine to address. Real love does not drain your peace or steal your identity; it strengthens you both. The truth is that sometimes walking away is an act of love, too, because it allows both people the space to heal and become who they are meant to be. The work is never just about holding on. Sometimes it is about learning when to let go, so that what remains is honest, grounded, and free of the bangarang that once clouded it. It becomes more than just emotion; it becomes strength, a reminder that the best things in life are worth the hard work it takes to keep them.

READER'S REFLECTION:

1. What does "effort" look like in the relationships that matter most to you?
2. When have you expected a connection without truly investing the time or understanding its needs?
3. How do you respond when love feels difficult? Do you pull away or lean in?
4. What role does communication play in keeping your relationships healthy and honest?
5. How do you balance your own needs while still showing up for the people you care about?

6. Have you ended a toxic friendship? How did you feel after the pain subsided?

Journaling Can Be a Reflective Tool

I hope that journaling is something you can take away from this book. Writing down my thoughts and feelings has become one of the most valuable tools I have. Throughout this entire process, it has helped me tell stories, uncover truths, and capture memories I might have otherwise forgotten. When I look back at the things I have written, I can see both the good and the lessons I needed to learn. The past does not define who I am now or who I will become, but it often gives me guidance on where to go next.

Most of us share everyday struggles, even if we rarely talk about them. We all carry experiences that shaped us, but fear of ridicule or judgment often keeps those stories buried. What I have learned is that honesty, especially with ourselves, is where healing begins. I am fortunate to have someone in my life I can talk to about anything, both the good and the bad. We trust each other enough to speak openly, even when the truth is uncomfortable. Aside from us, I have learned to be careful with what I share and when. Once something is out of Pandora's box, it cannot be put back in. Sometimes it is better to keep specific thoughts private until I am ready to share them.

Journaling allows that privacy. It gives me a safe place to release what I am not yet ready to say out loud. There is no judgment on the page, no expectation, and no need to filter my words. It is just me, being honest with myself. That kind of honesty builds clarity. It allows me to see where I have been, how far I have come, and what still needs work. Writing has been my mirror, my memory, and my quiet form of therapy. If nothing else, I hope that those who read this find the courage to do the same. Sit with your thoughts. Write them down. Find peace in the process.

I have come to realize that everyone is living their own life, carrying their own thoughts, stress, and perspective. It is easy to forget that. We all have bad days, and sometimes those bad days push us into moments we later regret. A quote attributed to Anthony J James and Ziad K. Abdeln: *Three things you cannot recover in life: the word after it is said, the moment after it is missed, and the time after it is gone.* That truth reminds me to slow down and think before reacting, even when emotions are high.

For me, journaling became one of the most effective ways to process those moments. It is my space to write freely without judgment, to spill out whatever I need to release. Sometimes I use it to make sense of what I am feeling. Other times, I write to get the noise out of my head. Not everything I put on paper needs a deep reflection or grand meaning. Sometimes it is just about creating space. When I look back at old entries, I can see where I have grown, where I made mistakes, and where I still need to work on myself.

Writing helps me examine situations such as my past relationships, the bedlam I witnessed, and the friendships I had to let go of. When I revisit those memories through journaling, I ask myself a few hard questions. Could I have done something differently? Did I ignore what was right in front of me? What lesson was I supposed to take from it? Each answer helps me understand not just what happened, but who I was in those moments. Journaling has become more than an outlet for me. It is a mirror that helps me see myself clearly, even when the reflection is uncomfortable.

Past Relationship:

Could I have moved and made it work?

I am sure that I could have, but I would have had to sacrifice everything I wanted to do. I did not want to move to a metropolitan area, and she would have been my primary focus. Relationships built on that imbalance rarely end well.

Am I in Love, or in love with being in love?

There is a difference. I was in love with being in love. She was not my soulmate. After a few brutal days, I started thinking things through and realized I cared for her but did not love her. It was the feeling of having an intimate person in my life. She was my first long-term intimate relationship.

How did she make me feel towards the end?

She was distancing herself and starting to pull away. The one thing that stood out to me is that she went to the Beer Gardens at her school, and I told her I got off early so I could hang out. I told her I would meet her, but she wasn't there. I tried calling a few times. No answer. The next day, I spoke with her, and she ended up staying at a house two blocks from mine. Her phone died. As things turned out, it was at her future husband's college apartment. They were only friends at that time. So, that really changed my mind. Maybe I could have kept trying, but what would it have helped? I would have been in a shitty, loveless relationship, could have been cheated on, and still would likely have broken up. That night was a pivotal factor in my decision to move on.

What vibes was I getting from her friends and family?

It was standard, albeit a bit awkward, because she always had family or friends around. Towards the end of the relationship, I was waiting for her to get home from work, and her roommate talked with me, foreshadowing the relationship. She wanted to move back home near her family, and she didn't want me to uproot my life. I, of course, tried to ignore it, but she was telling me things she knew.

You take anything you write, and it may help you see things that you may have missed. I also like to put things into other people's perspective. Take the second half of that chapter, where I talked about my friend and his poor life choices. I also used this to decide what I wanted to do. I asked some questions, not necessarily about his relationship, but about our friendship.

Friend with a drug and relationship problem:

Is the friendship mutually beneficial?

We just hung out on occasion for the most part. I had fun when we hung out, but it was mainly because of having beer goggles on. I quit drinking and did not want to be around alcohol, but that is all he wanted to do. I wasn't aware of the drug problem at that time. It put pressure on me when he drank, but I did not mention it. I told him I wasn't drinking, but he would still do it. We didn't do much besides hang out and kill time.

Were there problems with the friendship?

Yes, a few. He was using meth, and I had already dealt with enough drugs in my life through my biological father, and did not want that near me. His former partner, who created the drama with him, has been at his new apartment. He wanted me to stop by, but I was afraid she would stop by while I was there and cause drama. I do not want to be involved in other people's domestic issues, especially when it comes to someone attacking another.

He called me one day, and he was on something, and it wasn't alcohol, and he started berating me for not coming to visit him in his new house. He told me, "I was not a friend," and I explained my reasons above, telling him I did not want to be part of it. I told him I would talk to him later when he makes sense. He then started sending me angry and erratic texts. I finally had enough and stopped all communication with him. I had to block him to get him to stop.

Is this reparable?

At this point, no, until he decides to change his life. Now, I feel bad for turning my back on someone, but I need to distance myself from that environment.

Did I make any mistakes?

I probably didn't spend as much time with him as I should have, but it wasn't productive; we just hung out. According to a few people who stopped talking with him as well, his temper and drug use had been getting worse for a while. I initially distanced myself from him after the cops showed up at the place where we both had worked, and he was arrested for domestic violence with a previous girlfriend. A period of time passed, and I started talking with him again, before this last set of incidents.

What pissed me off was that I recommended him for that job. I was part of the leadership team, and I vouched for him. Reflecting on the friendship, I never mentioned that incident at work, but he didn't last long in the job. Sometimes, when you are writing things like this, other items that you forgot might contribute to your decision. I try to remember that things can be revisited at any time and are subject to change. It just helps you with your decision-making sequence.

Journaling enables us to reflect on our experiences and capture our thoughts. It is also valuable when you want to go back and analyze what you have written or compare and contrast decisions you may wish to make. Most of the stories in this book were ones I started writing to help me think through things, figure out issues, and even use writing as an outlet.

Journaling has shown me that healing is not about rewriting the past; it is about understanding it. Writing things down gives a chance to see how far I have come and where I still want to go. Some entries might bring back pain, while others remind us how strong we have become. The point is not to make every page perfect, but to keep turning them. Each word written is a step toward a better version of yourself. When you look back and realize that the person who once felt broken is now writing their own story, that is growth worth being proud of.

REFLECTION:

I have learned that life is full of choices, and they do not always come easy. The constant noise and pressure of deciding what comes next can be overwhelming. Journaling has become the tool that slows everything down for me. When I write, I give my thoughts room to breathe and settle. It is where I can untangle emotions that feel too heavy to carry and see the patterns that shape my decisions. Writing helps me process what I could not say out loud and understand what I really feel beneath the surface. It is not about grammar, structure, or sounding wise. It is about honesty and clarity. Putting my words on paper helps me find direction when everything else feels uncertain. Through journaling, I make better choices. It is not because life becomes easier, but because I can finally see things as they are, rather than how fear or stress tries to twist them.

READER'S REFLECTION:

1. When was the last time you sat down and wrote purely for yourself and not for anyone else to read?
2. How does putting your thoughts on paper change the way you process emotions or decisions?
3. What patterns or realizations have you noticed when you revisit what you've written over time?
4. How might journaling become less about fixing yourself and more about understanding yourself?
5. If you wrote one honest page today, what truth would you finally put into words?

The "C" Word

No, I am not talking about that "C" word. I am talking about the word that devastates many families around the globe. I am talking about cancer. This is one of the most devastating words in the human language. As soon as it is explained, everything around you pauses. The background noise fades, and a heaviness, a sadness, and a silence fill the room. Thoughts start racing, and emotions start bleeding through. Unfortunately, there aren't many medical options. Either try to treat it or live your days with it until the end. Even with treatment, sometimes the prognosis isn't necessarily good. There are natural ways to treat it or prevent its spread. I am not here to tell anyone what works or what doesn't, because that depends on the person's response, how widely it has spread, and the direction they want to go. They are making strides toward cures for the different types, but wouldn't it be nice if they identified the actual root cause?

Of course, smoking, chewing, drinking, or any other unhealthy lifestyle will put a person at a very high risk of cancer. But what about the people who don't do any of that or don't have cancer in their family history? Does the food we eat, which contains trace amounts of pesticides, fertilizers, herbicides, and other chemicals, have a significant impact on it? That question could fill a whole library of books, taking you down the rabbit hole of root cause analysis. I am not going to discuss that; I am going to talk about the effects of cancer on the family and share a few stories of the people I know who fought the fight.

At first, most people don't want to tell anyone about it when they're diagnosed. They don't want to hurt others, don't know how to start the conversation, and are still processing it themselves. Once the dust settles and the shock wears off, they may confide in close friends. Then eventually, it gets out, and when your name comes up for some reason, the "C" word follows. People will feel bad for you and experience a sense of mourning even when you are not there. My dad's stepdad passed away from liver cancer. I wasn't informed until his dying days.

I got to speak with him for a bit, but it was a conversation I really didn't want to have. There was not much said; all I heard was him writhing in pain and saying, "It hurts, it hurts," with heavy groaning. Within the next week or two, he was gone. My grandma was devastated by the loss. Shortly after his passing, she suffered a collapsed lung, had it fixed, then it collapsed again. She was a mess once he passed and didn't want to live anymore. My aunts and uncles honored her wishes as she didn't want another surgery, and she passed away peacefully. I wish this were the only story I had about cancer. But there were others. I have had people close to me with throat, lung, breast, pancreatic, and colon cancers, as well as lymphomas.

My grandma on my mother's side was diagnosed with throat cancer. She used to drink heavily and quit later in her life. It could have been that, but I am pretty sure it was from chain-smoking. Growing up, I used to dread visiting their apartment. The blue-gray hue of smoke hung in the small two-bedroom space. She would have two or sometimes three cigarettes lit at once while she worked on puzzles at the dining room table. When the company came over, they joined the smoke-a-thon, and it felt like you were breathing through a straw because of how thick the air was. I still remember the lump on her neck; it was the size of a softball.

Picture a frog with its vocal sac full. That was what half of her neck looked like. They ended up removing her esophagus, part of the jawbone, and part of the tongue. I can't remember if more was removed, but anything taken from you is too much. She ended up with a stoma in her throat. She didn't use an electrolarynx but had a patch that went over it, and it sounded like she was talking through a burp or a fart. Most of the time, she just wrote things down. She lived for many years after that, but it really wasn't a life worth living. She had to eat only blended food, had phlegm come up through the hole when coughing, and needed the stoma cleaned out all the time. My mom often did it whenever we visited. They moved to a house near my mom so she could better care for them. Eventually, they had to move into assisted living because they were too much for my mom to care for, and there were a few falling incidents. My grandpa's hips were so bad that he could only shuffle an inch or two at a step, and there were half flights of stairs at both entrances.

The last two I want to talk about are Bonnie's parents. Bonnie's dad passed away from lung cancer in 2009. She was the only person in his life who helped take him to appointments and cared for him for the five years he battled cancer. He had only been back in her life for ten years, so half of that time was spent watching him slowly deteriorate from the man she once knew to a shadow of his former self. If he hadn't been extradited from Tennessee, he wouldn't have received her number, and he likely would have died alone. Bonnie was afraid to help him because of how he hurt her mom, but she did what she felt was right. She could have easily walked away and done nothing, but she has always had an inner drive to help. Whether she was feeding animals or raising money for them, or helping people in need, she was always there for others.

Unfortunately, Bonnie's mom just finished chemo and radiation for small-cell lung cancer in 2025. She had a tumor in her lung, but it spread to the lymph nodes. The good news is that the cancer didn't grow. The bad news is that they called off the surgery because it had spread outside of the lungs. She is now going through monthly immunotherapy treatments through her port. It isn't specifically for small-cell lung cancer, but they are trying it to see if it can extend her life. For those unfamiliar, it is a brutal ordeal. Her mom is one tough woman, going through everything and still maintaining a positive outlook on life. One thing that has helped her feel better is juicing and taking an immunity juice Bonnie showed her how to make. She's been doing it every month and feels a little better, but she's still a shell of her former self and often gets tired. A side effect of either the cancer or the treatments has been extreme hot flashes that last for hours. When Bonnie first found out, she was wrecked. She didn't want to lose both parents to lung cancer. At the time of this writing, her mom is doing well and remains reasonably healthy.

Regrettably, she will likely succumb to cancer as it was not caught in time and metastasized

When I watched the people I love go through cancer, it changed how I see life and time. It stripped away all the small stuff I used to care about and made me focus on what actually matters. It showed me that strength isn't just surviving, it's also showing up, helping, and loving people even when it hurts. Cancer forces you to slow down and pay attention. It reminds you that moments are fleeting and that kindness, patience, and connection carry more value than anything else we chase in life. I've learned to stop waiting to tell people what they mean to me. I say it now. I make it known. Because one day, I might not get that chance again.

Cancer takes a lot from people, but it also teaches lessons that stay with us. It reminds us to slow down and love harder. It shows us that time is not guaranteed and that the people we share it with matter more than anything else. I have learned to tell the people I love how much they mean to me while I still can. I hope others do the same. Life is short, and it can be painful, but it remains beautiful when we pause to appreciate what we have. One last thing — **FUCK CANCER**. It ruins lives and families and puts people into financial ruin.

REFLECTION:

Cancer has taught me more about life than I ever wanted to learn. I have watched people I love fade, fight, and sometimes survive, and each experience left a mark on me that time cannot erase. It forced me to see how fragile life really is and how easily everything can change in a single moment. I learned that love is not just about being present when things are good. It is about showing up when everything feels unbearable. I used to take time for granted, assuming there would always be another visit, another conversation, another day to say what I needed to say. Cancer took that illusion away. It showed me that tomorrow is never promised, and that every word, every hug, every moment matters more than I ever realized. I do not look at life the same way anymore. I try to tell people how I feel when I feel it, and I try to notice the small things that make each day worth living. The "C" word will always carry fear and loss, but it also reminds me to live fully, love harder, and never wait to show up for the people who matter most.

READER'S REFLECTION:

1. What emotions come up when you hear or think about the word cancer?
2. How has illness, your own or someone else's, changed the way you see time and priorities?
3. What does courage mean to you when life feels uncertain or fragile?
4. How do you support others when words don't feel like enough?
5. In what ways can gratitude exist even in the presence of fear or grief?

Death at a Funeral

The death of a loved one is one of the most traumatic events we will ever face. Death is undefeated. It does not negotiate or show mercy, and it comes for everyone, no matter how good, kind, or prepared they may be. We are all born, and we will all eventually die. It is the one truth life never lets us escape. No amount of money, prayer, or planning changes that. When it is our time, it is our time. This chapter is about the people close to me, the moments I have watched them leave this world, and the strange, uncomfortable silence that follows. It is about the shock that doesn't sink in until days later, and the way a room full of people can feel completely empty. Death doesn't just take the person we love. It reshapes everything left behind. The world looks the same, but it no longer feels like it. There is an emptiness that lingers, a reminder that something once bright has gone out.

There are five stages of grief: denial, anger, bargaining, depression, and acceptance. When someone close to me dies, it changes everything for a while. I find myself walking through those stages, sometimes in order, sometimes all at once. It is painful and messy. Eventually, time dulls the sharp edges, and I learn to live with it. That does not mean I do not still get caught off guard by random thoughts or memories that hit out of nowhere. When that happens, I let myself feel it. I know now that the people I have lost would not want me to stop living or drown in grief. They loved me. They would want me to keep going and to remember them for who they were, not for how they left.

The dark side of death emerges when the glue that holds a family together dissolves. I have seen it more than once. Siblings drift apart after their parents pass. Tension builds over possessions, heirlooms, or even burial arrangements. It is already hard enough to grieve, and then this chaos piles on. Everyone's emotions are raw, and simple conversations can explode into full-blown arguments. At the time of this writing, I still have one grandparent living. My mom, my stepdad, and most of my aunts and uncles are still here, too. But the check is in the mail for all of us, and eventually that statement will no longer be accurate.

Death has a way of dragging out the worst in people. My grandparents did not have much, yet before the bodies were even cold, I remember family members rummaging through their things. It felt like vultures picking at the scraps of roadkill. I wish I could say that was rare, but I have seen it happen more than once. When there is money or other valuables, people start acting strangely. Everyone thinks they deserve something. My belief is simple. If you are going to have your hand out, it should have been out to help them while they were still alive. I have learned to expect nothing. That way, I will never be disappointed. If something good comes out of a tragedy, it is a gift, not an entitlement.

If my mom and stepdad want to live their best life, I will be happy for them. If they decide to get old and run naked through the vineyards of Italy, I really hope they throw some clothes on before we visit. They worked their asses off and sacrificed more than anyone I know. They deserve to enjoy their next chapter however they choose.

The thought of losing them is unbearable. They are two of the people I love most in this world, besides my wife. Even thinking about it brings tears to my eyes. When that day comes, I will gather every ounce of strength I have to get through it. I imagine trying to speak at their funeral, and I doubt I will be able to hold it together long enough to finish a sentence. I have been lucky so far. Most of the losses I have faced were expected, giving me time to say goodbye. But I know that will not always be the case. Sometimes death does not give warnings. Maybe that is for the best. I do not want to see it coming.

If there is one truth I have learned, it is that death hits everyone differently. It can bring out love, but it can also bring out bitterness and greed. The only thing I can control is how I handle it. I try to be patient, even when people around me lose themselves in anger or selfishness. I forgive where I can. If I reach out to someone and they push me away, I let them be. At least I tried. Sometimes space is what they need, and I respect that.

Grieving takes time. It is personal, messy, and unpredictable. There is no script. Sometimes we ugly cry, snot bubbles and all. We might not want to do it in public, but if that is what needs to happen, then so be it. This process is individualized. No one else can live it for us. If someone wants to be there to help, I am grateful. If they do not, I honor that too. Death is unfair, but it is also a rite of passage that we all have to face.

When someone passes, the most respectful thing we can do is pause. Their life deserves more than a scramble over what they left behind. I have seen people lose their dignity, treating a loved one's death like a clearance sale. It never ends well. The best way to honor someone is with grace, not greed. Sit with their memory before touching their things. Let the dust settle. Make decisions from compassion, not impulse. The way we handle what is left says more about us than about the person who is gone.

Death reminds me how fragile life really is. It strips away everything that does not matter, leaving only what does. The people I love will not be here forever, and neither will I. That truth could break me, but instead, I try to let it guide me. I tell the people I love how much they mean to me while I still can. When my time comes, I hope they remember me as someone who lived fully, laughed often, and loved deeply. That is all any of us can really ask for.

REFLECTION:

Losing people I love has taught me that grief never entirely goes away. It just changes shape over time. At first, it's sharp and raw, and I can feel it in every breath. Then, slowly, it turns into something quieter but always there, waiting in the background. I have learned that death is not just about loss. It is about learning how to live with the emptiness it leaves behind. I used to think grief was something to get over, but now I know it is something I carry with me. It has taught me to slow down, to pay attention, and to love harder while I still can. It showed me how fragile people are and how strong love can be. I try to focus on the memories instead of the pain, because that is what keeps the people I have lost alive in some way. I remind myself that I am still here for a reason. My story isn't done yet, and I owe it to those who can't be here to live my life in a way that honors them. Every loss has changed me, but it has also made me more grateful for every moment I still have.

READER'S REFLECTION:

1. How do you process loss? By holding it in, expressing it, or finding meaning in it?
2. What have you learned about life from saying goodbye to someone you loved?
3. How do grief and gratitude coexist for you when memories resurface?
4. What unspoken words or emotions still linger from someone you've lost?
5. How has loss changed the way you show up for the people who are still here?

The Bad Touch

eader's Note: The following chapter discusses childhood sexual abuse. While I have chosen not to include graphic details, the subject matter may still be painful or triggering for some readers. My goal is not to relive what happened, but to share how I faced it, forgave, and found my way back to healing. If you have experienced anything similar, please know you are not alone. This chapter is written with care, honesty, and hope for the child I once was, and for anyone still searching for peace. Please pause, step away, or skip sections if you need to protect your own well-being.

I hope no one ever has to go through something like this. Sadly, many already have. I also acknowledge that my story may not be as painful or as graphic as what others have endured. Everyone's experience with abuse is different, but the pain behind it remains the same. Pain is not a competition. Healing does not depend on how severe the trauma was. It depends on how deeply it altered your life and how you found your way through it. This isn't just an isolated tragedy. It's something that has become far more common than the numbers will ever show. Why do I say that? Because the key word is *reported*. Not everything gets reported because people are afraid or manipulated into not speaking up.

According to the World Health Organization (WHO), the statistics may vary, and it is estimated that 1 in 6 males and 1 in 3 females globally have been sexually abused. The truth lives in the silence. It lives in the shame that keeps people from speaking. It lives in families or among people who were close to you, where the unthinkable happens behind closed doors, and no one ever talks about it. It doesn't have to be family. It can be a boyfriend, a girlfriend, an acquaintance, or a complete stranger. Researchers acknowledge that these numbers are estimates because many people never disclose their experiences. There are many reasons someone doesn't report it. Whether it's fear, manipulation, shame, guilt, avoidance, or uncertainty, some victims don't remember until years later because they've repressed the trauma.

For me, those numbers are not just statistics, but they are part of my story. I was molested by my uncle when I was somewhere between six and eight years old, when the two events happened. He was ten years older than me. I don't remember exactly when. It happened in my grandparents' small two-bedroom efficiency apartment. I was lying on an uncomfortable, military-style fold-up cot in his room. What I do remember is being scared by the banging noises the radiator heater and pipes made in the old apartment. Sounds that came straight out of a horror movie before the monster showed up. Little did I know that should have been my warning that a monster really was coming. He invited me to join him in his bed, and I ended up crawling into bed with him because I was scared. That's where it had happened. I won't go into details here, for both your sake and mine.

My mom and I only stayed in that apartment a couple of times when we came back to visit during that timeframe. After that, I never wanted to stay there again and would instead stay with my other grandparents. I told everyone it was the cigarette smoke that bothered me, but it wasn't just that. I didn't feel safe. My uncle had a slight cognitive disorder, but that doesn't mean it was the reason this happened. Some people are just sick. I didn't understand that when I was a kid, and I didn't even grasp its gravity until later in life.

Years later, when I was an early teenager, he asked me if I remembered what we had done and if I wanted to do it again. I told him no. I told him what we did was wrong and should never have happened. I remember feeling instantly sick to my stomach when he said that, not just because of what he asked, but because it brought everything back. I still remember the look in his eyes when I told him. He just stared blankly and stopped talking. I'm not sure whether he realized it was wrong or stayed quiet because he didn't want to get in trouble.

For years, I stayed silent. That is where I held the most regret. What if my silence caused someone else to bear this burden? I was more afraid for them than for myself. Sadly, I kept it in because I didn't know how people would react or if they would even believe me. That's one of the most complex parts about something like this. When you do talk about it, not everyone believes you. Some may change the subject, look at you differently, or not want to process what you've told them. That's not for you to decide. You can't choose how someone will feel about it, nor should you worry. Holding it in is worse than letting it out. I didn't tell anyone until I was in my late twenties. When I finally did, I had already carried it for too long. It was initially met with resistance, but eventually it was accepted. I told some family members. I didn't tell my grandparents (his mom and dad) about the incidents. I don't think they would have processed it very well.

I decided to forgive what had happened, but the forgiveness wasn't for him; it was for me. I did not deserve what happened. Forgiveness doesn't mean forgetting or excusing the events. It simply means I've chosen not to let it control me anymore. It made me realize how abuse can become cyclical if it's never confronted. If the repetition of abuse is not broken, we can never really move on.

He passed away in 2022. I went to the funeral. I didn't feel much. I wasn't angry, but I wasn't sad either. I was just numb. I think that's what happens when something like this takes a piece of you long before the person is gone. You stop feeling anything for them. Death is usually the time to reflect on your memories with that person, but I didn't have much I wanted to reflect on when he passed.

Talking about this isn't easy, but silence wasn't going to help me heal. It only buried the pain deeper. The truth is, we never fully get over something like this; we learn to live differently. We take the power back piece by piece. For me, that started with forgiveness and the decision to speak openly about it. If you've been through something similar, please know it wasn't your fault. You didn't deserve it. You didn't ask for it. You are not alone. Healing doesn't erase what happened, but it reminds you that your life is still yours to live. You still have a future, you still have purpose, and you still have a voice. That voice is where the healing begins.

REFLECTION:

For years, I carried the weight in silence, thinking that not talking about it would make it easier to forget. Silence doesn't erase pain; it buries it until it grows into something heavier. When I finally spoke about what happened, I realized that telling the truth wasn't about reliving the past, but it was about reclaiming it. Forgiveness didn't happen overnight. It came slowly, through acceptance and through understanding that what happened was wrong, but it no longer had the right to control me. When I look back now, I see a scared kid who deserved protection and an adult who finally learned to let himself move on. Healing didn't come from anger or revenge. It came from honesty, from letting go, and from learning to live again without shame. If sharing this helps even one person feel less alone, then the pain that once broke me has finally found its purpose. The purpose is not only peace but also the power to protect others through truth.

READER'S REFLECTION:

1. How has silence or secrecy shaped the way you carry your pain?
2. What does healing mean to you when the hurt came from someone who was supposed to protect you?
3. How have you reclaimed your sense of safety, trust, or self-worth after betrayal?
4. What would forgiveness, not for them, for yourself, look like if it simply meant releasing the gravity of what happened?
5. How can sharing or acknowledging your truth become an act of strength instead of shame?

Start the Healing Process

Many things happen in life, and most of the time, we keep moving from one thing to the next. We stay busy because it feels like progress, but healing does not happen while we are running. Sometimes we need to stop, sit in the silence, and give ourselves time to process what has hurt us. It is good to keep the mind occupied, but eventually, the pain we avoid catches up. I once heard the saying that if you never heal from the person who cut you, you will bleed on the person who didn't. That is the truth. If I don't deal with my past trauma, it bleeds into everything around me. It colors the way I love, the way I react, and the way I see myself. Just as grief has stages, healing does too. Awareness, acknowledgment, acceptance, grieving, forgiveness, reconnection, and moving forward. The last two are where the work gets real.

Forgiveness is a two-part process. It means forgiving others and forgiving myself. That second part has always been more challenging. The mind is a cruel replay machine. It loops every mistake and replays every bad decision like a highlight reel I never asked to see again. I can forgive others, but forgiving myself has taken years of work. If I want forgiveness from others, I must ask for it with sincerity. That does not mean I will always get it. I have to be prepared for silence. Some people will never forgive me, and that is their choice. I have learned to respect that. It stings, but it is out of my control. If I keep making the same mistake, that means I have not learned anything.

I had a friend who meant a great deal to me. He made a mistake that landed him in prison for eight years. When he got out, he needed a sponsor, and I stepped up. I was the only one who agreed to be that person for him. It allowed him to attend events, work, and slowly rebuild his life. After a while, he met his future wife, and we drifted apart, but he asked me to stand up at his wedding. We started planning the bachelor party. We wanted to keep it simple, like a fishing weekend or golf trip, with just the groom and the groomsmen. I even said, "Anything but tubing."

Plans changed. At the last minute, it became a coed trip, and his fiancée decided everyone would go tubing. My wife is terrified of water, and I was furious. I had made that clear from the start. What bothered me more was that my wife wasn't invited to the bachelorette party, even though she thought of his fiancée as family. I was hurt and reacted poorly. I backed out of the wedding a few months before the date so they would have time to find someone else. I was angry and selfish. I went through every stage of the healing process after that. Looking back, it was their day, and I should have handled it better. Still, he never acknowledged my feelings or the effort I had made for him after prison. That part stuck with me.

Eventually, I reached out to apologize. I did not get a response, and I had to accept that. Some bridges cannot be rebuilt, and that is okay. I learned from it. I grew from it. Everything in life is either a blessing or a lesson, and that one was both. For a long time, I used pain as an excuse to fail. It became a built-in justification for why things didn't work out. That is the easy road, by blaming anything and everything except myself. It took me a long time to understand that accountability and forgiveness go hand in hand.

Part of my healing has been breaking the pattern of self-protection. For years, I would emotionally pack up and leave before someone else could hurt me. I would abandon people before they had the chance to. Even in relationships, I walked away the moment something felt difficult. That was a trauma response. I built walls around myself to stay safe, but all they did was keep me lonely. It took time and hard truth to realize that what happened in my childhood was not my fault. Those things happened to me, but I did not cause them. I was just caught in the fallout.

Forgiving myself has been the inflexible part of it all. I have failed more times than I can count, but every failure shows me what I still need to work on. None of us is perfect, and we were never meant to be. The best we can do is keep trying. Healing is not clean or linear. It is messy, raw, and painful. There were times I drank myself numb because it was easier than facing reality. I told myself it was temporary, that I deserved the escape. But escape always comes with a cost. I woke up with my head hanging over a toilet, mouthwatering, sick in the shower, wondering how I ended up there again. I hit rock bottom more than once. I numbed everything rather than face it. I buried my emotions instead of dealing with them. Rinse, repeat.

Healing is not a one-time event. It is an ongoing process that demands patience. Some days, I feel like I have it figured out. Other days, the past sneaks back in and hits like a freight train. That is normal. The key is not to stay there. When the old memories resurface, I breathe, acknowledge them, and move forward. The scars remain, but they no longer bleed. Healing is not about pretending the pain never happened. It is about learning to live with it, to find peace even when the past whispers in your ear.

True recovery begins when I stop running and face myself. Healing is not about forgetting. It is about forgiving myself enough to keep growing. It is about choosing peace over punishment and learning that survival was never the goal. Living is.

REFLECTION:

Healing has never been a single moment for me. It has been a long and uneven road that I still walk every day. Starting the healing process took courage I didn't know I had. It meant looking at the pain I spent years trying to bury and admitting that it was still there. It meant being honest about my own wounds and forgiving myself for the ways I tried to hide from them. Healing is not about pretending things never happened or erasing the past. It is about finally choosing to stop carrying it alone. Some days, it feels heavy, and some days, it feels lighter, but each time I face it, I find a little more strength and peace. Beginning to heal was not a single decision I made once. It is a choice I keep pushing every day to grow, to forgive, and to let myself move forward with a little more freedom than I had before.

READER'S REFLECTION:

1. What does "healing" mean to you right now? Where do you think it begins?
2. When have you mistaken numbing or distraction for healing?
3. What small act of care could you give yourself today that would move you closer to peace?
4. How do you know when it's time to stop revisiting pain and start rebuilding?
5. Who or what reminds you that you deserve to heal, no matter how long it takes?

Adapting to Change

As the old saying goes, change is inevitable. Change often looks good on paper when you're listing pros and cons, and convince yourself that you are making the right move. The truth is, no matter how carefully you plan, change will still test you in ways you didn't expect. Sometimes it opens doors, sometimes it knocks you flat on your ass, and sometimes it does both at once. The real lesson isn't just in making the decision, it's in how you respond when things don't go the way you hoped.

After nearly seven years with a great company, I received a random call from a recruiter interested in interviewing me for a new role and seeking my expertise. I interviewed, and it went really well. I was told they would offer me the role, but I had to wait for budget approval. Six months later, I literally received an email with an offer letter that was significantly more than I was making. I discussed the opportunity with my wife first, and then conducted a pros and cons analysis to consider changing my career.

Changing from Company A to Company B:

Pros:

1. ~$25,000 pay increase (life-changing for us).
2. One business segment vs two to manage.
3. 45-hour workweek vs. 55-hour workweek (salary for both).
4. The benefits are better.
5. Keep the same 3 weeks of vacation (remember this is ALWAYS nego-

tiable).

6. Vacation increases by 1 day every year after 5 years.
7. No further growth potential in Company A.
8. Opportunity for a GM position in under 4 years for Company B.

Cons:

1. Leaving the people I worked with, an outstanding culture.
2. Would get 4 weeks of vacation in year 12 from company A.
3. Commute goes from 25 minutes to 33 minutes.
4. Move to a new position of Production Manager.
5. Have to set up all the production for a new facility.

Any way you slice it, there were not enough cons for me to stay. The last two seem like a lot, but not really. I had employees, a supply chain, customers, and upper managers. This new role eliminated the supply chain aspect and allowed a focus on a single business segment rather than two.

After I made this decision, I realized I had overlooked some of the cons, and the pros were not as true after I joined. So I made a career mistake based on listening to the hiring manager's falsehoods about the role. I had to adapt to a significant change of leaving a job before finding another one. I was putting in 65 plus hours a week, and my mental health was deteriorating. Well fuck, I am a moron. The good thing is I talked this through with my wife. I had also been looking for jobs before I put in my notice, and I was getting calls. I was planning to leave this company and had taken some steps to soften the blow. Below is a list of things I did to help us survive during my time without employment.

1. I refinanced my vehicle loan and reduced my payment by over half. I made minimum payments until I found work, and then returned to my regular payment amount before the refinance. This allowed me to pay off more principal per month and finish paying it off a few months faster.
2. I put two loans in forbearance. This allowed me to have six months off

from payments without affecting my credit score. Not that this is the best option, but you must do something when your back is against the wall. Two bad things happen: the loan is longer, and interest accrues during the pause. Most permitted loans are non-lien-style loans. For vehicles and mortgages, the banks can take your assets and put your loans in default, so avoid falling behind on them.

3. I was also squirreling some survival money for months. I managed to save up $20,000. I know some people would say, "Why didn't you pay something off?" I was concerned about a prolonged job search. I planned six to nine months in survival mode.

4. I paid off all my credit cards, so I didn't have to worry about high interest rates. I also avoided using them unless completely necessary. This is for emergency use only! Racking up credit card debt will quickly deplete cash flow.

5. I canceled anything that wasn't necessary. This was easy for me; it was the Wi-Fi and cellphone I needed to keep. I needed to be able to email and communicate with hiring managers or recruiters. I cut the cord on Netflix, cable, and anything that wasn't a necessity.

6. We stopped making any unnecessary purchases. You cannot keep your lifestyle without half of your income coming in. I avoided the good-old Amazon binge-spending sprees.

7. I was lucky I was on my wife's health insurance, but that may be an issue to plan for if needed. I would not feel comfortable being without it, but typically, there is only one open enrollment period per year. Timing could play a role in this decision.

8. I knew my 401(k) allowed hardship withdrawals, but I considered them a last resort. It comes with taxes and an early withdrawal penalty, so if I had taken it, I would have paid those right away. Life was stressful enough, and I didn't need another hit from the IRS later.

9. I also considered taking a 401(k) loan. The good part is that I'd pay the interest back to myself instead of a bank, but it's still not free money. Payments start almost right away, and it's easy to fall behind. It's a short-term option, not a solution.

10. I had a bunch of things that were collecting dust. I was able to sell some things to make extra cash.
11. I also started giving plasma 8 times a month. It can be $600-$800 per month in income. It is not much, but it can help with groceries or some bills.
12. There are numerous temporary jobs, including farm help. I am lucky enough to have a family farm, and I worked there as much as possible.
13. I reached out to a few friends to see if they needed help with anything. I learned that you never really know until you ask. When I did help, I gave it my full effort because that's what they deserve.

Here are a few things I did and considered doing during this time. Change is hard. This was a challenging time, and I had to adapt and make changes; otherwise, I would have faced significant difficulties, adding more stress to an already stressful situation. You do not want to end up like the couple in *Fun with Dick and Jane*. You should think outside the box and explore alternatives, but always consider the consequences before taking action. It is always better to have something else lined up before you put in notice, but I was at my breaking point.

Change has a way of revealing our character when plans fall apart and comfort fades. It forces you to look in the mirror and decide whether you will complain or adapt. It is not always fair, and it is rarely easy, but it has a purpose. Every change I have faced has stripped away something I thought I needed and replaced it with something I actually did. Sometimes that lesson comes through failure, and sometimes it comes through growth. Both are teachers if you are willing to listen. Change is not about what you lose; it is about what you discover while rebuilding. When you can look back and see how far you have come, you realize that every hard turn, every risk, and every setback shaped you into someone stronger, more capable, and more self-aware. That is the quiet reward that comes after the storm.

REFLECTION:

Change has never been easy for me. It has a way of shaking everything I thought was steady and forcing me to see what I am really made of. I used to fight it, clinging to what felt safe and familiar even when it no longer fit the person I was becoming. But the truth is that growth does not happen in comfort. It occurs in the moments when everything feels uncertain, and I have to trust myself enough to take the next step anyway. Change has taught me that adaptability is not about losing who I am. It is about finding new strength within myself when life shifts in ways I cannot control. Each time I have faced change, I have discovered a version of myself I did not know existed. I have become someone stronger, wiser, and more capable than before. I no longer see change as an ending. It is the next step toward becoming the person I am still learning to be.

READER'S REFLECTION:

1. How do you typically respond when life shifts in a way you didn't expect?
2. What changes in your life were hard at first but ended up leading to growth?
3. How do you know when to hold on and when to let go?
4. What helps you stay grounded when everything around you feels uncertain?
5. What would it look like to see change not as loss, but as an invitation?

Don't Go Scorched Earth

U nless you are born into a family with money, chances are you are like the rest of the people in this world. We have to work for what we want in life. I wasn't given a silver spoon, but I was given a key to unlock any door I chose to open. I look back on my youth and am grateful for having grown up on a farm. It instilled a strong work ethic, and there were days when you worked from sunup to sundown. I think of that when I see some people I have worked with; they punch in and punch out, putting in enough effort and care not to be fired. If that is what they want to do, that is their prerogative. I am not wired that way. I have found that this is the key to achieving success in life. Now, I am not saying work yourself to death, but I am saying put in the extra effort.

Looking back on my career, one thing that has helped me is going above and beyond. In any leadership role, I understand the importance of having a team that goes above and beyond. When people do that, they end up with higher compensation, better opportunities, and a stronger rapport with team members. Unfortunately, there are limitations to that. Advancement is based on open roles, newly created positions, and budgets. This means that, as an employee, we may need to be patient or look for our next role. If it is a great company, there is an exercise called succession planning. This exercise helps identify and develop the next generation of leaders within that company, enabling them to prepare for their future roles. The positive aspect is that the workforce is aging and will soon be retiring. Most managers will communicate their plans to us and have training plans in place; if not, we can discuss where you want to be. If we are what they are looking for in a leadership role, they will set a path forward for us. If they do not, then other roles elsewhere may be necessary.

I think effective communication when you approach a manager is crucial. I had a recent employee who was very blunt, didn't work well with others, and, if she didn't like someone, wouldn't even acknowledge their existence. Do not be like this person. This behavior is a fast track to nowhere, or worse, termination. Employees need to be coachable and approachable. She was a very hard worker but lacked the soft skills (communication skills). She was recently in a scuffle, and I needed help in a department. So, to remove her from the issue, I hired her and made her a lead. As I mentioned, she was a very diligent worker, and I needed help setting up a department. She took it on with no hesitation. I didn't spend much time working with her in the past, but she was always friendly to me. I always try to say hi to everyone and make sure I call them by their name, and I didn't have any issues with her.

She did, however, have an issue with another employee in another location, and worse still, his brother was also his boss. That was the fundamental issue. It is an awful practice to have family in charge of family, as that can create favoritism and nepotism. That was why I wanted to get her out of that environment. At first, there were no issues, but the company asked her to fill in the area where the toxic environment was. That team was like the *good ol' boys club*; if one didn't like you, they all didn't, and they all banded together. I myself had run-ins with the employee mentioned earlier. I would say hi, and he would ignore me 9 out of 10 times. One day, he came in and was up on the back of a truck because he was a company transport driver. He started going off about my employee (my new lead), because she thanked everyone except him. I asked her about it, and she said I refuse to acknowledge him. I found this to be an opportunity to coach and mentor. I brought up an experience from my past and asked her to kill them with kindness. Take the step and go out of your way to be nice and give greetings. For me, it felt like I was living in their head rent-free, and I learned not to care what people thought about me. The response I got from her is that I will never acknowledge him because of what he said. I let it be at that point, as she was not going to attempt to make amends.

The next Incident had a domino effect, affecting four employees and leading to their job losses over the next two days. She ended up filling in for the department manager and had to interact with the employee she had been ignoring. She called me and stated that when she called another department. The employee who was there and the guy she was ignoring answered the phone, said her name, and started laughing. She immediately called me and told me about the situation. She was upset and started crying. I went to the location and wanted to talk to her in person. It was another opportunity to coach and mentor. I wanted to discuss this in person versus over the phone. When we spoke, I told her to document what happened. Still, I said, "There wasn't really any context given, and they could have been joking about something else and continued laughing about something else after her name was mentioned. That was hard for me to justify."

I ended up calling HR so that they would be aware of what was happening. Well, in that time frame, he had been heard swearing and saying, "Fuck this place, fuck that, and fuck everyone." These things led to his termination at the end of the day on Tuesday. On Wednesday morning, his brother, who was his manager, brought back the terminated employee's uniforms and ended up throwing them at a manager. He had thought that she had reported him, and that is why he got walked out. When I walked past him, he threatened me to keep her away from the department, and too many F-bombs came out to track. I actually had to call and intercept her to prevent her from coming into work, so that we wouldn't have any further escalation. I had her wait at a local restaurant, and he was terminated early that morning. Another transport employee immediately resigned because he didn't want to work with her, even temporarily.

I sat down with my employee and discussed what had happened. This was another opportunity to coach and mentor her, as she was making new requests and demands of other employees and wanted management to demand an apology from another employee before she would help the department. At this point, the leadership team and HR sat down with her, and she unloaded on the HR person for "not doing anything". Side note: Disciplinary discussions are private, and other employees should not be informed about disciplinary actions taken against them. This wasn't good enough for her; she wanted a public tongue-lashing for being wronged. I do not know what happened, as this was before she was my employee. The two items she wanted apologies for were from months prior, and she just wanted management to force the apology to assert dominance. She was terminated for insubordination due to what she said to the HR manager. I purposefully left that out. One manager in the meeting said, "She scared the shit out of me." It wasn't for what was going on; it was for how she approached and addressed people. She created the toxic environment around her.

We will have bad days, and someone may call us out for a mistake. It is imperative to investigate, communicate effectively with the person who made the mistake accusations, and bring it up for discussion. If I had needed an apology every time I was blamed for a mistake, I would be a miserable person and would have to wait a long time.

We must also be professional above all, and the workplace is so diverse, with people of different sexes, ages, religions, races, and ethnic backgrounds. People will not always see eye to eye. I felt that she was not coachable or approachable. That is the problem at hand. I would have put up a stronger fight for keeping her, but the risk wasn't worth the reward.

Working hard is essential, but how we handle ourselves when things go wrong matters even more. We can be the best workers in the building, but if we lack self-control, respect, or humility, it will eventually catch up to us. The real test of character isn't how we act when things are easy. It is how we respond when we feel wronged or overlooked. I have learned that no job, no title, and no paycheck is worth losing your integrity over. When we walk away from a situation, we want people to remember our effort, not our anger. Never go scorched earth, because once the dust settles, we still have to live in the ashes.

REFLECTION:

I have learned that hard work alone isn't enough. The way I approach it matters just as much as the effort itself. I've seen people chase results so fiercely that they burn every bridge around them, leaving nothing but scorched earth where opportunity once stood. I've done it myself at times. I have pushed too hard, taken things too personally, and lost sight of the bigger picture. Real success isn't about being the loudest or the hardest-driving person in the room. It's about knowing when to push and when to pause, when to stand firm and when to listen. It's about earning respect through consistency, not fear. I want my work to reflect integrity, not ego, and my legacy to be built on the people I lifted up, not the ones I stepped over. When I walk away from something, I want the ground to stay intact, not burned behind me. That, to me, is the real measure of hard work done right.

READER'S REFLECTION:

1. When has your drive to succeed crossed the line into self-destruction or burnout?
2. How do you balance ambition with rest and recovery?
3. What does "working hard" look like when it's healthy and not fueled by anger or exhaustion?
4. Have you ever burned bridges or relationships in the name of progress, and what did that teach you?
5. How can you pursue excellence without losing sight of balance and compassion?

Believe in Yourself and Set Goals

Depending on your support structure in life, you may or may not have heard the words, "I believe in you." For some people, that phrase never comes. Not everything is a Hallmark movie, and not everyone knows how to say those words. I was fortunate to hear them from my wife, usually when I was at a crossroads or considering a career change. She has always been supportive, and I am grateful for that. Still, I have learned that the most important belief is the one I hold in myself. Not everyone grows up with encouragement or validation, but even without it, believing in myself became the key to stepping outside of my comfort zone.

It took years to develop self-confidence. For a long time, I was faking it. I put on the mask and pretended to have it all together, but inside, I doubted everything about myself. I was not worth much. I did not believe I deserved anything good, and I constantly felt like a burden. In my late teens and early twenties, I was lost, trying to figure out my purpose. Looking back, I realize most people feel that way when they first start their independent lives. Some call it depression. I called it angst. It was that uneasy sense of not knowing where life is headed, but knowing something inside is restless and ready for more.

That inner strength, which psychologists call self-efficacy, does not appear overnight. Life throws obstacles and setbacks along the way, and those never disappear even after reaching a goal. Life rarely moves in a straight line. It feels more like a series of waves with peaks and valleys that test everything we know. At some point, I had to sit with myself and ask what truly makes me happy, what kind of life I want to build, and what type of career would align with that vision.

Some people dream of staying home to raise a family, and there is absolutely nothing wrong with that as long as it is a mutual choice. It takes understanding between partners. If one person wants to build wealth, travel, or chase ambitious goals while the other prefers a simpler, quieter life, it can create friction. I have learned that mismatched ambitions can breed resentment. It goes both ways. I have been the hyper-driven one before, wanting to push forward when someone else was content to maintain, but it never ends well. Suppose two people's paths do not align; no amount of forcing or shaping changes that. The healthiest decision might be to find someone whose goals complement mine.

I had to learn that I am the driver of my own happiness. No one else can hand it to me. Once I figured out what I wanted, I had to translate that vision into goals. Goal setting became the framework for everything I have accomplished. The most successful people I have met share that trait. They do not drift. Their goals are clear, measurable, and grounded in purpose.

If I wanted to become a CEO, for example, that would be a great aspiration, but it is not a plan. There are only two ways to get there. One is to start my own company. The other is to be appointed to lead someone else's. That means understanding the space between where I am and where I want to be. What does it take to earn that position? What skills, education, or experiences do I need to get there? The first step was always the same. Investigation. I learned to study openings, compare requirements, and look for patterns. That built the foundation for everything that followed.

Once I knew what I wanted, I began to evaluate what I lacked. I asked myself the hard questions. Do I have the skills they are looking for? What am I missing? I would make lists and start filling those gaps one by one. It could be leadership experience, industry-specific knowledge, or advanced education. I found opportunities that aligned with my goals and started working toward them. It took time — often longer than expected — but every step forward counted.

In every company, there are internal projects that require extra hands to implement change. I started volunteering for those. People usually led the teams in positions I aspired to, so it became a chance to learn from them and show initiative. The key word was volunteer. If I had ever responded with "I am not paid enough for that," it would have been career suicide. I learned early that the people who advance are the ones who consistently go beyond what is asked without demanding instant rewards. Effort always pays off, maybe not immediately, but it does eventually.

There were times when my goals required formal education. Executive leadership programs, for example, can be expensive. If a company saw alignment between my growth and theirs, they would often cover the cost. If not, I would save and pay for it myself. The first step was simple. Register, commit, and follow through. From there, each course became its own goal. Study, prepare, test, and repeat. Completing that one milestone always led to another. It was never about instant gratification. It was about stacking wins.

I used to believe success was about talent or opportunity, but I realized it is more about endurance. Staying focused when things are uncertain. Showing up when I do not feel like it. Finishing what I start. Every role I have ever taken has tested my stamina.

Attitude also plays a massive role. I used to carry a negative perspective tied to frustration about where I was in life rather than where I wanted to go. I envied people who seemed unbothered, who could let things slide off like water on a duck's back. Meanwhile, I would stew in my emotions, sometimes with a twelve-pack or two pints of ice cream. It did not fix anything. Eventually, I learned that failure was not personal. It was a signpost pointing to growth.

I will never forget the time another manager nominated me for an Operations Manager position. When the owner heard that, he called all the managers together. It should have been exciting, but when I walked into that meeting, it turned into a public humiliation. The owner told me, in front of everyone, that I was not ready and would fold under the pressure. The sad thing is, no one looked me in the eye the whole time this character assassination went on. The two other leaders who backed him up were the same two who would later be fired due to their toxicity to the culture within the company. Still, it stung. I walked out feeling humiliated, angry, and embarrassed. It would have been easy to quit or become bitter, but I did not.

A year later, that same company came back and asked me to take over a failing division that had been run into the ground. I could have said no out of pride, but I saw it as a chance to prove something, not to them, but to myself. I worked relentlessly. Sleepless nights. Long days. Rebuilding processes, retraining staff, and taking ownership of every issue. Over time, the numbers turned around. I proved my worth, but, more importantly, my capability.

When another company reached out with an offer that recognized my value, I took it. I left on good terms, even though the old company tried to keep me with counteroffers. I had built strong relationships, but it was time to grow. I heard later that the owner was furious with himself for not creating a path for my advancement. That made me smile, not out of spite, but out of validation. It showed me that my effort had not gone unnoticed.

Still, I left the right way. I called the VP personally to explain, gave my two-week notice, and wrapped up everything I could before leaving. HR later told me they appreciated the professionalism. I have learned that no matter how ready I am to move on, leaving the right way matters. Burning bridges might feel satisfying in the moment, but it limits future opportunities. I would rather be remembered for my integrity than how I exited.

Looking back, I see how belief and goal-setting are intertwined. One without the other is incomplete. Setting goals without believing in myself leads to frustration. Believing in myself without setting goals leads to drift. The two balance each other.

When I reflect on my journey, I see the pattern clearly. Decide where I want to go, break it down, and take it one piece at a time. As the old saying goes, *How do you eat an elephant? One bite at a time.* My elephant happens to be massive. Each bite, each step, builds discipline. Over time, I have learned to appreciate the slow grind. Instant gratification never lasts. Real growth takes time.

My goals keep evolving. Every time I reach one, another appears just ahead. Sometimes I joke that I must be a glutton for punishment for enjoying the challenge, but truthfully, it is the pursuit that keeps me driven. Other people might want peace, or family, or balance, and that is perfectly fine. Everyone's version of success looks different. What matters is that it is honest.

Believing in myself has never been about arrogance or pretending to have all the answers. It is about trusting that I can learn, adapt, and rise again after every fall. Goals give me direction, but belief gives me the strength to keep walking when the path gets hard. Setbacks do not mean failure. They mean progress is happening. Every lesson, every no, and every small victory have shaped the person I see in the mirror today. Confidence is not something that appears when life gets easy. It is something I have built, one goal, one mistake, and one small step at a time. I stopped waiting for permission or validation. I believe in myself enough to keep moving toward the life I was meant to create.

REFLECTION:

Self-belief has become the foundation for everything I have accomplished. Without it, I would never have taken the risks that changed my life or faced the moments that tested me the most. Believing in myself has not always come easy. There were years when doubt and fear felt louder than confidence. Over time, I learned that belief isn't about eliminating those doubts. It's about choosing to move forward even when they are still there. Setting goals gave me something to reach for, but believing in my ability to achieve them gave me the endurance to keep going. Each step forward, no matter how small, built momentum. Every setback reminded me that growth takes patience and resilience. I no longer wait for permission or validation to chase what I want. I trust that I have what it takes to keep building, learning, and becoming stronger.

READER'S REFLECTION:

1. What's one goal you've put off because you doubted your ability to achieve it?
2. How has self-doubt influenced the choices you've made or the chances you didn't take?

3. When was the last time you felt genuinely proud of yourself, and did you let yourself celebrate it?

4. What does belief in yourself look like in action, not just in words?

5. How can setting goals become less about pressure and more about purpose?

Decide Your Journey

The only constant thing in life is change. Right now, my life is far from perfect. I sometimes need a change or a fresh perspective, like seeing things through a different lens. I remind myself that this is my journey, not anyone else's. If I have a wife, kids, or family, they come along for the ride. When things fall apart and life hits hard, it helps to have people who genuinely have my back. When I do not, I have to remind myself to reach out to someone. I tend to close myself off, like many people do, thinking I shouldn't burden anyone with my self-inflicted problems.

I have learned that nothing is embarrassing about therapy. If someone does not want to join me in my process, that often says more about them than it does about me. Sometimes healing is lonely work. It is what I want and need to do. When the struggles involve relationships, therapy becomes a tool for understanding, not blame. I had to stop seeing it as a weakness and start seeing it as an investment in my own peace.

Everything in life can change for the better. I began creating lists of the things I wanted to change and worked on them step by step. I had to remind myself that no one else would do it for me. Building a routine became the foundation of progress. A healthy routine, repeated daily, eventually became a habit. And that mattered.

Not all habits are good ones, though. I have learned that the hard way. Shopping, gambling, drinking, and drugs are all traps that give temporary relief and lasting regret. Even sex can become destructive when used as a weapon or an escape. The key is to develop healthy habits. The things that build instead of destroying. Walking, working out, biking, hiking, or even making the bed every day, exploring a new town, attending a show, and creating small anchors that bring me back to life when things feel heavy. Routine is powerful because it keeps me moving forward, even when my emotions drag behind.

When I started school again, my routine saved me. I worked ahead whenever I could so I could take time off if needed. Once I finished, something strange happened. I began having nightmares that I was missing classes or failing exams. My brain had become so used to structure that it panicked when it stopped. The routine had become part of me. But when it was gone, I filled the void in unhealthy ways. My drinking increased, and I fell back into patterns that numbed instead of healed. That was when I realized how dangerous habits could be, either good or bad, because they all grow from repetition.

When I disliked where I lived or felt trapped financially, I had to take action. Nobody was going to save money for me. I started researching how to manage debt and get ahead. I learned to pay off the smallest debt first, then roll that payment into the next one. It is incredible how fast progress builds once momentum starts. I had bad debt, a single income, and nine years of school behind me, but I started small. One bill at a time.

Before long, I was paying off loans faster, and I began to see light at the end of the tunnel. I started making $1,600 payments a month compared to $550, and I will pay off my truck three years sooner. My next goal is to pay off my wife's vehicle, then put that money toward the mortgage. It takes discipline and sacrifice. I stopped spending money on things that did not serve me. I sold unnecessary toys and focused on needs instead of wants. Sometimes that meant cutting back to the bare minimum and living on ramen for a while, working extra hours, or taking a side job. The older I get, the more I realize the price of waiting. Making changes is easier when energy is still on my side.

Career changes come with risk. Sometimes it turns out to be a mistake, but I would rather find out from experience than wonder what if. I never leave one job without another lined up, except for the one time I discussed, and that will not happen again. Not everyone needs to know about my plans and confidentiality matters, especially in workplaces, as gossip spreads like wildfire.

I learned to update my resume regularly and write a separate cover letter for each position. I joined LinkedIn and built a network. I started connecting with headhunters and executives, posting about topics that mattered in my industry. I stopped chasing tiny raises and started aiming higher. Companies love it when people accept small offers, but I have always believed in asking for what I am worth. I set a number in mind before applying, and if a company could not meet it, I kept looking.

Some jobs required degrees, and I accepted that. A two-year degree opens doors in the trades or some management positions. A four-year degree opens doors to more business-related positions or management roles. Leadership classes and continued education keep me sharp. Every bit of knowledge adds to my value. If I am going to invest my time and money, what better investment could there be than in myself?

Health is another part of this journey. My wife battled SIBO and IMO for two years. She was miserable and spent thousands on doctors who gave her no answers. We turned to homeopathic medicine, and she began to improve. The pills were not covered by insurance, of course, because that system profits from customers, not cures. Watching her fight made me think about my own health. I am not in bad shape, but years of drinking have added weight, and age does not make it easier to get back into shape.

Through it all, my wife became an expert on her condition, and I learned alongside her. We did our own research, compared notes, and found better solutions than most of the doctors provided. I have no medical credentials, but I can say this: Do not stop looking for answers when it comes to your health. Sometimes you have to fight for your own life, as no one else will.

Relationships also play a massive role in well-being. I had to take a hard look at who was helping me grow and who was holding me back. Toxic relationships, whether family, friends, or partners, can destroy mental health. I had to learn when to let go and when to seek help. Counselors and therapists are not just for crisis moments. They can help navigate change and rebuild strength.

As I look at my life, I ask myself one question. What do I want from this journey? Life is long, and time never slows down; it keeps moving at the same rate. The older I get, the more I feel that illusion of time speeding up, but it is me slowing down. The only way to fight it is to make each day count. Small steps turn into big ones.

At the end of the day, this journey is about progress, not perfection. I will fall. I will fail. I will lose direction sometimes. But every step forward still counts. No one is coming to save me, and no one can walk this path for me. That truth used to feel harsh, but now I see it as freedom. It means I hold the power to change my story. I keep building habits, taking chances, and making choices that move me closer to the life I want. I learn from my mistakes and forgive myself faster. I stay humble, keep growing, and focus on forward motion, no matter how slow it feels. My journey is my own, and it is worth every single step.

REFLECTION:

Life is not just about survival. It is about creating meaning along the way. I have learned that I can get so wrapped up in routines, responsibilities, and expectations that I forget to stop and ask what I truly want from this journey. It is easy to lose direction when everything feels urgent or when I am too focused on taking care of everyone else. But when the noise quiets, I am left with the one question that always matters: Am I living with purpose or just passing time? Clarity about what I want gives me control over where I go. When I take the time to define my goals and understand what fulfills me, I make choices that align with my values instead of reacting to life as it comes. My journey is mine alone, and it is still unfolding. I may not always have the answers, and I will make mistakes along the way, but I am no longer content to drift. I want my days to mean something. I like the steps I take to lead somewhere intentional. When I stay true to that, I stop surviving life and start living it.

READER'S REFLECTION:

1. What do you want your life to feel like, not just look like, as you move forward?
2. When you imagine your future, what values or experiences matter most to you?
3. How often do you pause to check if the path you're on still aligns with who you're becoming?
4. What lessons from your past are worth carrying with you, and which ones can you finally set down?
5. If you could redefine success for yourself today, what would it mean?

Starting Over

There comes a time when we realize that holding on to the past is just another way of staying stuck in it. We all like to think we can fix what's broken, patch up what fell apart, or somehow rewind time to before things went wrong. Starting over doesn't mean pretending the past never happened. It means learning to live with it, accepting what you can't change, and building something better with what's left.

For me, starting over has happened more than once. I've had to rebuild after losing things I thought were permanent. I've changed jobs, career paths, relationships, who I trust, and even parts of myself. When life hit hard, my first instinct was to hold everything together, even when it was already gone. I remember leaving a job that had become toxic, not because I wanted to, but because I had to choose peace over a paycheck. That was one of the first times I truly started over. It was terrifying. I had built an identity around being strong, reliable, and unshakable. Walking away from that version of myself felt like a failure, but it was actually a sign of personal growth.

Starting over also meant learning how to live differently. After years of drinking to numb pain and silence my intrusive thoughts, I had to face myself honestly for the first time. There's nothing comfortable about confronting your own reflection when you've been avoiding it for so long. Facing it gave me clarity. I learned that healing isn't about forgetting or fixing everything. It's about accepting the person you are right now and allowing yourself to move forward. There were times I thought I had it all figured out, only to realize I was starting from zero again. When my personal life fell apart, I had to learn to live alone, to trust myself again, and to find purpose in something other than what people thought of me. I started walking every day to clear my head. I began journaling to make sense of what I was feeling rather than burying it. It also helped me look back and understand how I truly felt during those times. Those small steps didn't look like much, but each one became part of my recovery.

There was a point in my life when everything seemed to collapse in a cascade. Work, relationships, and even my sense of direction all seemed to fall apart. I remember sitting in my car after leaving my job for the last time, wondering what was left of me outside that building. For years, I had measured my worth by what I could produce or provide. Starting over forced me to measure my worth by something more profound than what I did for a living. I had to measure it by who I was when everything I built was gone. That realization hurt at first, but it also saved me. It also means forgiving myself, not just for what I've done, but for what I allowed when I didn't know any better. I can't move forward if I'm still carrying resentment toward my past self. That version of me that endured everything deserves compassion, because without that, I wouldn't be here now.

When I decided to return to school and learn something completely new, I was okay with being a beginner. At some point, we were all there. When I started tech school, there was a diverse group of people from young to old. Everyone there had a different story about what was happening in their lives, and I'm sure many of them were starting over, too. I had spent long hours working for little pay and felt underappreciated, stuck in my current situation. I still remember the day I walked across the stage and received my master's degree. It put my life into perspective and filled me with an overwhelming sense of accomplishment. That is something that we appreciate when we fight for it. I know a few people who went on to the military. It was amazing to see how different they became after completing basic training and as they advanced through the ranks. Everyone has a distinct sense of accomplishment that drives them, and finding that helps with setting a direction.

There will always be moments when you question whether you are strong enough to begin again. I've felt that too. I remember sitting in an empty apartment, wondering how everything had changed so quickly and if I had anything left to offer. Each time, I found that the smallest steps forward were enough. A new routine. A walk outside. A call to someone I trusted. Little things reminded me that I wasn't finished yet. If you're standing at that point right now, tired, uncertain, or afraid, remember this. Starting over doesn't erase your story. It turns the page. It is proof that your story is still being written. This is your story, and *YOU* are the main character.

REFLECTION:

Starting over takes courage because it means having faith in something that can't yet be seen. It asks me to trust myself again after being hurt, disappointed, or broken down. It isn't about perfection; it's about persistence. Every new beginning asks me to let go of a little more of the past and believe that what's ahead will be worth it. I've learned that starting over doesn't mean forgetting who I was. It means embracing who I am becoming. It means thanking the version of me that carried me this far and giving the next version permission to take over. I can't stay in the same chapter and expect a different ending. Life doesn't always go according to plan, but it always gives me another chance to begin again. Real peace comes when I stop asking "why me?" and start asking "what's next?" That's where my strength begins.

READER'S REFLECTION:

1. What does "starting over" mean to you? Freedom, fear, or something in between?
2. When was the last time you permitted yourself to begin again without guilt?
3. How have past endings made space for something better in your life?
4. What beliefs or expectations do you need to release before you can truly move forward?
5. What would it look like to see starting over not as failure, but as growth?

II

Bonnie's Story

Bonnie's Story shares her firsthand account of domestic violence, survival, and healing. Initially written for a public domestic violence awareness piece, it's included here in her full voice to offer perspective and hope. These chapters may be difficult to read, but they aim to shed light on strength, recovery, and resilience.

Here is her story:

The Beginning

I am not entirely sure where to begin or how to tell my story, so here it goes. It nearly spanned three decades and would be unbearably long if I were to recount it in its entirety. I was with my abuser for almost twenty-seven years, that is right, close to twenty-seven years. It felt like an entire lifetime living a life of hell; I thought that I would never escape. I was prepared for this to be my life, or for it to be the end of it. Before I get too far into the story, I would like to give a brief snapshot of my childhood. There are many more stories I could tell, but those are for another time.

I had a tough childhood. My dad was an abusive alcoholic with drug problems. He was physically and verbally abusive. My mom loved us very much and did her best to take care of us as well as she could, given the limited resources she had. She always sacrificed for my brothers and me, and at times, she went without to ensure we all got what we needed. My dad convinced her to run away with him before she was even eighteen. She was young and naive and had a traumatic upbringing. When she was about eight years old, her mother's boyfriend hid in a closet, waited until her dad napped, and then shot him to death. She and her siblings were placed in foster care after that.

She went to a family with a farm. She ended up getting raped and mistreated by the farmhands. She met an attractive, smooth-talking young man with a southern drawl (my dad), who promised a better life, so she ran away with him. She ended up pregnant with me shortly after.

The next-born sibling after me passed away at 3 months old. My two living brothers are five years apart in age. The oldest is five years younger than me, and the youngest is ten years younger. We grew up poor, moved around a lot, and were even homeless, living in a car for just shy of two years. My dad had a warrant for his arrest for grand larceny theft. He went on the run, which meant we all had to do the same. That is why we lived in a car and were homeless for that long. He was caught. My mom, my brothers, and I came back to the Midwest. When we returned after the ordeal with my father, I started high school. I never really had many true friends because we were always on the move and constantly relocating. I was shy and insecure.

I had watched what my mom went through at the hands of my dad. Many times, throughout the years, often behind closed doors, I could hear the impact of his blows and her crying. As I got older, I tried to intervene, and I got shoved aside. He would reserve the belt or spanking for when we misbehaved. When he went to jail, I convinced my mom to divorce him. I swore I would never let ANYONE treat me this way ever! This leads into my story with my abuser. I will briefly touch on some key points over the years. As you read my story, keep in mind that for every violent, tragic moment I write about, there are many, many more untold. They all have left a deep emotional scar on my soul; the following are just a few that haunt me daily.

At sixteen, I was still very shy and insecure. I was teased constantly for being so extremely skinny, nearly malnourished. I felt inadequate, didn't fit in, never measured up, and never felt good enough. I never really had what one would call a "true boyfriend" or been on any dates; I just had innocent crushes. I met my abuser when I was sixteen. He was a smooth-talking twenty-three-year-old who always hung out with the next-door neighbors. I often sat on my front porch. He befriended me and would frequently come over to talk. He would tell me how beautiful I was. He was always flirty with me, talking about how much he admired me and how he would treat me if I were his girlfriend. He would also bring me little things, such as sodas, fast food, flowers, and a few dollars for my lunch, etc. My young mind was easily impressionable.

I continued to deny and discourage his advances. I only wanted to be his friend, but he was very persistent. My mom told me to stay away from him, saying he was too old for me. I should have listened. Usually, I was one of those good girls who listened to what my mom told me. I had dreams and goals. I was one of those little girls who wanted to be a model when I grew up. It was always my dream. Since my mom didn't want me to hang out with him, he found ways to talk to me. He would visit my school. He convinced me that he loved me, and we started meeting at places behind my mom's back, without telling her I was with him. I am not going to lie; I started to like him more than a friend. He made me feel special, loved, and important. As time went on, I eventually agreed to be his girlfriend. He constantly barraged me with sexual advances, but I never allowed more than holding hands or the occasional innocent kiss. I was one of those girls who wanted to save my virginity for the person that I would fall in love with, eventually marry, live together, and have kids.

I used to babysit two kids for the lady down the street for extra money. He would stop by when I was there watching the kids. We would hang out, watch movies, and kiss when the kids were sleeping. I liked kissing, and that was all I wanted to do, but he always tried to go further. One day, I was babysitting the baby, who was napping, and the young boy was not there. He came over that time and convinced me to go upstairs and watch movies in bed so we could cuddle. We cuddled and kissed, and before I knew it, he was taking off my shorts. I said no, but he insisted, saying it was just my shorts so that we could cuddle in our underwear.

I nervously agreed. We continued to kiss, then suddenly he rolled on top of me and pulled off my panties. I was shocked and firmly said no and tried pushing him off me in protest. I was seventeen, weighed ninety pounds, and he was twenty-four, six feet tall, and weighed one hundred ninety-five pounds. I continued to struggle to get him off me as his hands forcefully groped my body. As I continued to squirm beneath him to get away, he suddenly put both his hands around my neck, squeezed, shook me violently, and said, "Loosen up, bitch, and let it happen." I immediately froze with shock and fear. At that moment, he forcefully raped me. I felt so hurt, afraid, used, and so many other things to describe my emotions. He convinced me that what had happened was okay and that he had to help me overcome my fear of being intimate. He did this because he "loved" me. I tried to believe him and kept it a secret out of fear and embarrassment. We continued to see each other. Eventually, he convinced me to start skipping school to be with him. By this time, I was drinking and partying.

He then tried to befriend my mom to get closer to me. It worked. My mom liked to party and drink (reliving the days of her youth), and eventually, he was around my household more often. He eventually asked me to move in with him. I said no at first, but he persisted and wouldn't take no for an answer. Sick of the persistence, I talked with my mom, and she said, "Absolutely not." He kept pestering me to move in, and I didn't heed my mother's words. By the time I was seventeen and a half, I told her I was moving out and that she couldn't stop me. She tried just about everything to convince me not to do it, but he had me so brainwashed that I moved in with him.

My mom was so angry with me that she told me never to come back begging to move back in. She threw all my clothes in garbage bags and tossed them on the porch. I was heartbroken because my mom was my best friend. I knew those were words of an angry, desperate mother trying not to lose her baby girl. I understand this now, but back then, I took those words to heart. I swore for the life of me, no matter how hard things got, I would never come back. Over the years, things became increasingly complicated, but I never asked to return to her home. He had told me that his mother lived with him so he could help take care of her before I moved in, but after I moved in, it turned out to be untrue. He still lived at home with his mother. Looking back now, he isolated me from any sense of safety in my life.

REFLECTION:

Hearing Bonnie's story hit me hard with some of the childhood similarities we had. It's one thing to read about abuse, but it's another to know the person who lived through it and still found the strength to tell it out loud. The beginning of her story shows how early pain can twist what love is supposed to mean and how hard it is to break free once control takes root. What bothers me most is that she was still a kid trying to find her place in the world while carrying scars that no one could see. It made me think about how much people hide to get through the day, and how often survival becomes a habit before healing ever begins. Bonnie's courage to tell the truth about what happened to her is powerful because it shows that even when life challenges you, it can't take your will to keep going. That kind of strength doesn't come from being unbreakable; it comes from being broken and standing up anyway.

READER'S REFLECTION:

1. What parts of Bonnie's story resonate with your own experiences?
2. How does her willingness to be vulnerable challenge or inspire you?
3. When have you felt like you were involved in something that you didn't expect to turn out badly?
4. What does courage look like when life gives you a chance to rewrite your story?
5. How can you honor your own beginnings, no matter how uncertain they felt?

The Gaslighting Narcissist

I still remember the first time he hit me. It was within a week or two of moving in with him. We had gone to one of his friends' houses the night before to hang out, drink, and party. The next morning, while I was getting ready for school, he accused me of looking at one of the men at the party the night before. I told him I didn't. He wouldn't back down and kept saying I did. He called me a bitch, cunt, and a whore. Next thing I knew, he shoved me so hard that I went flying down the hall about six feet and fell. My schoolbooks went flying everywhere. The same feelings I felt in that bedroom when he raped me came back. How can someone who says they love me toss me to the ground like that? Something in my head told me I had made a colossal mistake moving in with him.

I grabbed my school bag and said I was leaving, never to come back. That made him even angrier. He grabbed my arm and shoved me against the wall and yelled, "You are not going anywhere bitch! Where the fuck are you going to go? Your mother doesn't even want you back!" Scared, stunned, and lost, I just fell to the floor and cried. I didn't leave that day. Looking back, God, I wish I had.

Still seventeen years old, he introduced me to cocaine, and I eventually became addicted. I was spiraling out of control and eventually dropped out of high school. We partied a lot. Things were not always bad. When he was nice, he was super friendly. Eventually, the mean would come back. He would tell me he was sorry and that I shouldn't make him so angry. It was always my fault for making him feel that way. I believed him. I had to beg him to let me get a job. He didn't want me around other people without him. We eventually got a place of our own. I started working a factory job to help pay our rent. We were always lacking money. He worked as a handyman and a seasonal worker, and occasionally took on cash jobs. I was the household's breadwinner.

I eventually mended ties with my mom, but didn't get to see her often. He kept very close tabs on me and always had to know my whereabouts. It was always an argument whether I wanted to see my mom or some friends. He wouldn't let me get my driver's license until I was twenty-one. I remember one time I convinced him to let me walk to the mall to meet up with my friend from school. She and I walked around the mall talking and reminiscing about old times. When I got home, I was bombarded with questions and accusations. Are you sure you were at the mall? Are you sure it was *only* my friend I met? It usually ended with him hitting me. After several similar situations, I found it was just easier not to leave the house than to try to prove where I was. I eventually lost my job for missing too many days due to having black eyes, split lips, or visible bruises everywhere. I felt shame and didn't want people to see me like this.

As time went on, he got more strategic and would hit me in places where the bruises were not visible. He would hit me in the back, chest, ribs, and mostly my head under my hair, and he would even brag, "You think I don't know where to hit you so that the bruises wouldn't show." I had so many swollen lumps on my head from his fists over the years. Between the lumps and his pulling my hair out, some days it hurt too badly to brush my hair.

Before I met him, I loved to do my hair and makeup to feel pretty. I did it religiously before school. Within a year of living with him, I eventually stopped that, as well. Whenever I did my hair or makeup, I was accused of trying to look suitable for someone else; again, it was easier not to. The only time I did was when he asked me to, so I wouldn't look so haggard.

When I was eighteen and a half, one day I looked in the mirror and didn't like the frail, 85-pound girl who was dying, both inside and out. I made the conscious decision to cut cocaine out of my life. I flushed it in the toilet and never touched it again. He did the same, surprisingly. Although I caught him doing it off and on in later years.

With a fresh lease on life, I landed a new job at a company. I loved working; it gave me a chance to get away from him for a while. I felt important, and it gave me a purpose. Unfortunately, he took the money from my paychecks. He was the "Man" of the house, so he made the rules and decided where the money went.

One of the several nights that sticks out in my mind happened a few years later. He told me to get ready and make sure I looked *pretty*, so I did. We went to a local bar. He told me before we went inside that he had little money, so do not ask for anything. Just sit there and look pretty. I had water, and after about two hours, he became belligerent and started embarrassing me.

He started telling a table full of men I didn't know about my body and my cute little ass. But I was so skinny and didn't have any boobs. He even had me stand up and turn around for them to look at me. After twenty minutes of this relentless humiliation, I whispered in his ear so that I wouldn't embarrass him, "I am leaving and walking home." We didn't have a car at that time.

On the walk home, I was passing a different bar and noticed my mom inside. I went inside, asked her for a cigarette, and then said hello. I was sitting next to her, talking for maybe fifteen minutes, when he came into the bar. I didn't think there would be a problem, he said hi to my mom and acted all nice. Then he whispered, "What the fuck do you think you are doing walking out on me like that and embarrassing me. You said you were going to the bathroom, and you snuck out! You are a fucking liar! Now I find you in another bar, you whore!" He then bit me on the cheek very hard for the next few seconds before releasing his bite. Yes, he bit me with his teeth on my cheek.

When he let go, he told me to tell my mom goodnight and to get up and leave with him; otherwise, it was going to get a lot worse. My cheek hurt so bad, and of course, no one around me even knew what had happened, so I got up and walked out with him. Once we were outside, he yelled at me with a slew of belittling words. He called me a lying bitch, a cunt, and accused me of whoring around at another bar. He thought we were out of view when he decided to shove me, throw me around, and hit me, but we were not. People from the bar came out to stop him, and my mom told me to come in with her. I knew from our history that it would be worse if I went inside. I told her I

174

was OK and left with him. All the way home, he yelled at me and shoved me around. At one point, he pushed me to the ground and kicked me in the ribs multiple times.

When we got back to our temporary home. Yes, temporary, as we were homeless again and staying with his brother and his wife. He proceeded to hit me several times right after he closed the door to the room. When he finished hitting me, he told me to get the fuck out. I didn't have anywhere to go at 1 AM, it was raining, so I asked him if I could go to sleep. He insisted that I leave, or he would kick my ass more, so I got up and left. Before I walked out, he told me to take my two cats and not to come back. I had no carrier, so I begged him to let them stay there until morning. He agreed, and then I left. I did not know where to go or what to do, so I figured I would try my mom's. She was still out at the bar, and a friend was over babysitting my brothers.

I knocked on the door, and she could see that my nose and lip were bleeding, and I was crying. My cheek and eye were starting to swell. I asked her if I could sleep there for a little bit. I lay there, but sleep was the last thing my mind was going to do at this point. I just lay there in pain, wondering, "What the fuck just happened to me? What am I going to do now?" This was the worst he had beaten me so far, and I thought it couldn't get worse. Looking back now, I was sadly mistaken.

I must have fallen asleep at my mom's. By early morning, my mom's friend woke me and told me, "You should leave before your mom sees your face because she would flip out". I walked into the bathroom and was in shock. The person looking back at me was battered and beaten, with my eye black and blue and swollen shut. My lip and nose had dried blood. My cheek was black and blue and swollen. You could still see the outline of his teeth sunk into my cheek. There was no lying or hiding what happened. It was so evident that I had been bitten.

Shortly before leaving my mom's, the phone kept blowing up. I didn't answer since I knew it was him. Eventually, I answered. He told me to come home now, or he was going to kill the two cats. He said he would snap their necks. I had no reason not to believe him because he killed two of my kittens years earlier. One kitten, he told me, got out of the door. He later admitted he snapped its neck because it scratched him. The second one: I came home one day and found the kitten lying there, its back legs sprawled, unable to move and barely breathing. He said he "accidentally" stepped on it; I still doubt that to this day. Needless to say, I went home again.

Several years passed with my daily life hyper-controlled by him, and he was obsessed with knowing my whereabouts at all times. He made me prove my receipts, what I could wear, music I could listen to, and how to cut my hair. At times, I wasn't allowed to work, and when I did, I had to give him money and show my check stub. I was constantly accused of cheating, and eventually, I stopped making eye contact with people for fear of accusations. When we eventually got cellphones, I had to answer mine right away if he called. If I didn't, it would be an argument or a fight. He distanced me from all my family and friends. I eventually had no friends and minimal contact with my family.

REFLECTION:

Bonnie's story from this part of her life was like watching someone slowly disappear while still trying to exist. The physical abuse was brutal, but the mental control was worse. It showed me how gaslighting eats away at a person's sense of truth until they question everything, even their own reality. What affected me most was knowing how young she was and how easily manipulation can wear the mask of love. He isolated her piece by piece, convincing her that she was the problem while he destroyed her confidence and sense of self. I've learned that emotional abuse doesn't leave visible bruises, but it can leave scars that take years to heal. Her strength in sharing what happened isn't just brave; it's proof that even when someone tries to erase your identity, they can't take away your voice once you decide to use it.

READER'S REFLECTION:

1. Have you ever doubted your own reality because someone convinced you that your feelings or memories were wrong?
2. What subtle signs have you learned to recognize when someone is manipulating or controlling the truth?
3. How do you protect your sense of self when others try to twist your words or experiences?
4. What boundaries can help you rebuild trust with yourself after emotional abuse?
5. What does reclaiming your voice look like after years of being silenced or dismissed?

The Abortion

In 1997, I became pregnant. I had been off birth control for about a month because he wouldn't allow me to spend the few dollars to get my prescription. Buying his beer was more important, and he was drinking more frequently. I had stopped drinking entirely several years earlier because I needed to be the responsible one, and I didn't want to have liquid courage to say something I shouldn't and start a fight. I didn't feel safe enough to not be of sound mind anymore. He was verbally and emotionally abusive every day, and that was his routine. He always put me down and even embarrassed me in front of others. He would shove me and scream at me and get right up into my face. There was always that eerie feeling that he could hit me at any time. That threat was always there, burning in my head. There was no predicting when he would snap. Typically, he got very physically violent towards me when he drank.

The hardest thing was that he put on a good fake front in front of most people. Only a couple who had witnessed it knew his capability. If you asked most people who knew us, they would say we had a great relationship and that he loved me very much. If they only knew what happened behind closed doors, their opinions would be drastically different. As some years went by, some got to witness his abuse, and most *men* didn't stop the beatings that happened in front of them. One of his go-to moves, other than beating me in the head with his fists (because the bruises wouldn't show), was to choke me. To this day, I have a hard time with anything that is snug around my neck. One of the several times, I remember him choking me out so bad that I thought I was going to die. Just before I blacked out, I could hear his brother, who was over, finally get off his drunk ass and say, "Stop before you kill her."

Anyway, back to being pregnant. I had been feeling very sick for about two weeks, and I was afraid to tell him I suspected that I might be pregnant. I finally got up the courage to tell him what I suspected and asked for money for a pregnancy test. Deep inside, I had always wanted a baby girl so badly. Even as a young girl, I dreamed of having one someday when I grew up. Unfortunately, I had already decided in my mind earlier that I did not want to bring a child into such a horrible, dysfunctional, abusive, and sick situation at all. Maybe someday, if he had changed, I could have had a baby, but not if he was the way he was. So, I was praying to God very intensely that I wasn't pregnant, but deep down I knew I was. I weighed 98 pounds, was 26 years old, and my body felt different.

Around that same time, he had started a new roofing company in my name to avoid child support. This situation will be brought up later in this story. He came home one day with a pregnancy test. He followed me into the tiny bathroom of the piece of shit 1978 fourteen-by-seventy-foot single-wide trailer we lived in. My heart raced with fear as I waited for the plus or minus sign to appear slowly. When the time was up, I checked, and my heart sank to the lowest pit of my stomach. I knew all too well the events that would unfold, as they had before.

I fell to the floor and cried, not a typical cry but an absolute bawl. He immediately started screaming at me, "Well, this is fucking great! You stupid bitch, this is all your fault! How the fuck are we supposed to afford a kid!?" I made an appointment with the doctor's office. I didn't have a job at the time because he had gotten me fired. I had no insurance and no car. The doctor confirmed I was five weeks pregnant. I was so heartbroken and scared. We didn't really talk about it for a while after I told him what the doctor said.

Part of me was excited, and I started daydreaming about hopefully having a baby girl or even a baby boy. Well, a few weeks went by, and he was drinking one night and told me I needed to schedule an abortion because we couldn't afford a baby. He was already a deadbeat dad for another kid from before I met him. He had a child at seventeen, which is why he wanted to work for cash on a seasonal basis. So, I didn't want to have this baby with him because of what he was, and a tiny part of me still wanted to abort the baby, but most of my heart was against it. I told him I didn't want to, and of course, a fight broke out again. He told me to "Just fucking do it." I was never asked to do anything; I was just told to do it. I also waited on him hand and foot like I was his maid for everything. Bring him what he wanted when he asked for it.

I called the next day, and an abortion cost $450. I told him that, and he became outraged. He said I would have to come up with the money somehow. The clinic informed me that it needed to be done as soon as possible, but no later than twelve weeks from the date of conception. As the weeks passed, I developed a noticeable baby bump. It became apparent almost immediately with my petite frame. I started to accept the idea of having a baby and being a mom despite my horrible home life. Whenever I got the chance, I would go to the thrift store and pick up cute baby clothes, just in case. I started a little box of baby stuff and hid it. I told no one I was pregnant, not a single soul. I remember him asking a friend for money so I could have an abortion, and his friend said no. In my heart, I felt relieved, in a way, because I was starting to grow attached to and love this tiny little human growing inside me, even though I was sick all day, every day.

I threw up all hours of the day and was nauseous and weak. Of course, another fight ensued because he wasn't getting the money and blamed me for getting us into this situation. He was screaming at me at the top of his lungs and started shoving me. He then yelled, "I will just beat that kid out of you, so you miscarry!" Then came an onslaught of hits. He spun me around and punched me in the stomach so hard I fell to the ground in pain. I lay on the ground in the fetal position, trying to shield the growing baby in my stomach, as he hit and kicked me several times.

We didn't come up with the money in time for the twelve-week deadline. At fifteen and a half weeks, he told me to lie, so I did. On April 16, 1997, I had an abortion. It was excruciating physically and emotionally. I threw up immediately after I sat up after the procedure. I cried all the way home. My heart was broken into a million pieces. I felt like the worst person in the world, and I still think God will punish me for what I had done. My family and friends never knew any of this about me. My husband knows, but to this day, my own mother still doesn't know this or many of the other things he put me through over the years.

REFLECTION:

This part of Bonnie's story was the hardest to read and even harder to imagine living through. It showed the kind of fear that strips away every bit of choice and replaces it with survival. I know how much this hurts her to this day, knowing she still carried love and hope for that baby, even when every part of her life told her not to. The way she was controlled, beaten, and forced into something no woman should ever face is beyond comprehension. But through it all, she still found a way to tell the truth about it, and that takes more strength than most people will ever have to face. This chapter reminded me that pain doesn't always end when the moment is over. It lingers in silence, in guilt, and in the things that never get spoken out loud. The fact that she can tell it now means she finally took that power back. That is what survival looks like, not with the absence of pain but the courage to stand in it and keep telling the story anyway.

READER'S REFLECTION:

1. What emotions come up for you when thinking about choice, loss, or what-ifs in your own life?
2. How has judgment, from yourself or others, shaped how you've processed difficult decisions?
3. What does compassion look like toward yourself or someone else facing a deeply personal choice?
4. How can empathy exist even when experiences or beliefs differ?
5. What does healing mean when the past can't be undone, only understood?

The Downward Spiral

In the coming months after my procedure, his daughter moved in with us full-time. Before that, he had her every other weekend on and off. I had been playing stepmom to her since she was about six years old. She was now almost fifteen. A few months later, I took in one of her 14-year-old friends. She was the neighbor's daughter, and her family was moving away. She wanted to finish school with her friends. So, I was trying to be a mom to two teenage girls, who were barely ten years younger than me.

I was working full-time at another factory at the time. I had to convince him to let me get a job because we could barely keep food on the table for the girls with his drinking and gambling. His violent outbursts were increasing in frequency and intensity. Sometimes he would go a few months without hitting me and only verbally abuse me, and sometimes it was multiple times a week. The verbal abuse was a regular daily occurrence. I was called stupid a lot, a dumb bitch, cunt, whore, lazy, etc. You name it, I've been called it. He did everything and anything to belittle and degrade me regularly. I had zero self-esteem left, and I mean zero. I was slowly dying inside and losing any hope that my life would be anything more than this. At this point, I wanted to leave him, but knew deep down my life would have been on the line.

By 1999, my brother fell on hard times, and I took him in as well. So now there are five of us living in a tiny trailer. My ex worked on whatever roofing jobs he could get. He would get paid and gamble the money away. I was the only one responsible for paying the bills. That same year, I started working a federal job.

Also, that year, I found out that my dad was extradited to Wisconsin for non-payment of child support in the fall, for all those years when we three kids were minors, and my mom was struggling to feed us and keep a roof over our heads. I had not heard from my dad since I was thirteen or fourteen, before he went to prison. I went to the court date with my mom to support her and out of curiosity. When I saw my dad, he looked tired and hopeless. The empath in me felt sorry for him. I passed a note to the bailiff with my phone number on it. I wasn't sure whether I wanted anything to do with him at this point. He was homeless, disabled, and had nothing.

He had told me that he had been sober for years. I ensured that he received the necessary help with clothing, food, a place to stay, disability assistance, and healthcare. He wasn't in good health. I found out that after he got his first Supplemental Security Income (SSI) disability check, he was back to binge drinking. I was disgusted, but he had no one else, so I felt that I needed to help him take care of himself.

In 2000, he was diagnosed with stage 4 lung cancer. I went to my dad's house daily to help with whatever chores or tasks he needed. I also took him to the cancer center for his chemo and radiation treatments. I was doing this while trying to work and provide for a family of five. I worked second and third shifts, caring for everyone's needs during the day, and slept whenever I could. My ex would scream my name and wake me up to fetch him a beer, even when I had to rest for work. Anyway, back to the story.

Soon after, we moved to a farmhouse that was big enough for all of us. We lived there for twelve years, and there are so many bad memories associated with the house that I still cannot bear to drive past it. Those were the years that hate overtook the last string of love. I had completely lost hope that he would change by 2002 or 2003.

During that stay in the farmhouse, he had thrown me down the stairs, put my head through walls, dragged me down the stairs by my hair, and shoved me out in the cold, stayed out all night, and cheated on me. This was a regular occurrence: beatings and verbal lashings. I was the one who paid the bills, and they were all in my name. He even made me pay thousands of dollars on his back child support payments so he wouldn't go to jail. That was after being threatened that if he went to prison, he would come out and beat or kill

183

me.

He was constantly yelling at me about something, whether it was that the house wasn't clean enough or when we were experiencing financial difficulties. It was always the same accusations. Why did I take so long at the grocery store? Why was I 10 minutes late coming home from work, etc.? I would have a panic attack if I were stopped by a train or caught in a traffic jam. One of the many times we fought, I don't remember what started this particular argument. He beat me up pretty bad again. I lost consciousness. He must have gotten scared because I woke up in the passenger seat of his truck. He was yelling that I was a "Stupid fucking bitch." He threw me out of the car at a mutual friend's house. I lay in the yard for a couple of minutes, gathered myself, and then went to the door at 2 AM. The next day, he blew up her phone, demanding that I get my worthless ass home. This was one of many hazardous situations I was placed in.

As the years went by, he drank more and more. It increased every night. He was battling type 2 diabetes and alcoholism. The complications from diabetes cost him opportunities to keep any roofing jobs. He wouldn't show up and would break contracts. Eventually, he just stayed home and drank. By 2006 or 2007, he said that I had to marry him so he could be on my insurance, because he would need it as he got older. I told him I wasn't going to marry him, that I begged him in the past to change, go to counseling, or treatment. He refused; nothing had changed over the years, and everything had gotten worse. I wasn't even intimate with him anymore, except for the few times he would basically force himself on me. Thankfully, he was so drunk all the time, and with the uncontrolled diabetes, he couldn't perform anymore, and of course, that was my fault too. He would scream at me constantly, "If I weren't fucking him, I must be fucking somebody else. Who was it?" I never cheated on him; I was faithful throughout the years.

He continued to badger me about getting married for the next year or two. I remember the night I gave in to marrying him. It was after he beat me up badly again. I received a cracked rib, dislocated jaw, and other bumps, bruises, and bleeding.

We got married in 2009. I know this is terrible, but when I said, *I do*, I didn't mean it. We had been together for twenty-two years by then. It was November 2009, and I was thirty-eight years old. When I look at photos from that day, I see myself as a shell of a woman. I looked so sad and vacant. I was so skinny from being stressed out all the time. I could never get over 103 pounds. He made me take out a loan against my 401(k) to cover the costs of this wedding. I did it as cheaply as I could, but I had to have the wedding he wanted. Even the color was what he wanted. I didn't have a say in anything. To this day, I despise the color royal blue and hate seeing it.

In 2009, I got a little Yorkie that I rescued to try to fill some of the void in my life and heart. My daily life was so empty, devoid of love, compassion, and cuddling. Although at this point, I didn't want him even to touch me, much less cuddle. I needed something to love and fill the void in my heart. He didn't want me to have this dog. I begged him. This little dog was named Dewey. He kept me going through the years. Some nights when I didn't want to go on, my little Dewey was there by my side to lick my tears. He would even try to protect me, as small as he was. He was my little emotional support animal.

In 2010, my ex had a minor stroke due to complications from not taking the steps to control his diabetes and his daily alcohol consumption. He could still walk and talk and function normally, but the stroke affected his balance and vision. He lost his peripheral vision in the stroke. Instead of taking his health seriously and making changes to his lifestyle, he continued his path of self-destruction with his daily drinking, chain-smoking, and drug use.

I eventually found out he was smoking crack when I found a crack pipe in the basement. He told me what he did was none of my business. He would steal bill money out of my purse for drugs or gambling. His drinking and violence were entirely out of control. He would always tell me he was dying and would die in five to six years due to his diabetes complications. He would always tell me that if I tried to leave him or called the cops, he would kill me. I always believed he would and was certainly capable of it. Now more than ever, I knew that he would follow through on the threat. He would tell me that he didn't care if he went to prison; he was dying anyway.

I could barely keep the bills paid, since he was always taking money from me for alcohol, cigarettes, drugs, or gambling. He would borrow money from people and tell them to get the money from me on my payday. Sometimes I would receive only $100 or $200 from my entire check. He demanded that he needed it for back child support.

One day, I was backing out of the driveway when two strange men approached me on both sides of the car and said that my husband had told them that I would pay them money for drugs. I said no and that I have nothing to do with whatever he owed them. This upset the men, and they started screaming at me. One of them showed me that he had a gun in his waistband. He said, "Bitch if you do not pay us, your husband said I can take it out of your ass. Thankfully, my neighbor heard them yelling at me and came out with his gun and told them to leave me alone. I went to work and couldn't get the events of the day out of my mind. I was used to feeling this way.

Unfortunately, when I got home from work, they were at my house hanging out with him, drinking, and smoking crack. I was forced to pay them the $300 he owed them. The sad thing is that none of this even surprised me anymore. He was so mean and selfish. He demanded that I wait on him all the time. I remember one time he insisted that I make him something to eat before I went to work, and he spat a mouthful of food in my face. He then threw the plate at me, all while screaming at me that it wasn't warm enough and tasted like shit. I would get yelled at regularly if something wasn't hot enough or if I forgot to put mayonnaise on his sandwich, among other things. I even had to prepare his insulin shots throughout the years. He would tell me how many units of each were needed. Sometimes I wished I had given him too much, ended his life, and regained my freedom.

My ex had tried to apply for disability due to his declining health. Well, he discovered that now that we were married, my income disqualified him. So now he decided that we needed to get divorced so he could get SSI disability benefits. He also said that we wouldn't really be divorced, it would only be on paper, for financial reasons. It was the end of 2011 or the beginning of 2012. I absolutely despised him. I hated everything about him. I hated how mean, evil, and selfish he was. I had seen this as a possible out for me. In my mind, my dream was to escape him and live my own life. I didn't know how I was ever going to manage that, but I was hopeful.

I started working a second job to get extra money and try to keep bills paid and get money to file for divorce. I worked third shift at my job at the time and then went straight to my second job with my brother-in-law. I would help clean up the ground of roofing debris, usually between noon and three pm. Go home and shower, sometimes I was black from head to toe, and try to sleep until I went back to work. He typically had people over and had the music loud on purpose, or yelled for me several times to bring him beer or run to get his cigarettes, or even give his drunk friends a ride.

REFLECTION:

My heart sinks as you can start to feel the hope slipping away, and that something better will never come. It shows the point at which survival becomes autonomous. Bonnie wasn't living anymore. She was existing. Every day was another round of control, humiliation, and exhaustion layered on top of everything she already carried. Even with everything, she still never gave up and kept struggling forward. She worked to keep a roof over everyone's head, cared for people who didn't care for her, and tried to hold together a life that kept falling apart. The violence had become normal, and that is what makes this part of her story so powerful. It shows how long someone can endure when they believe they have no way out. I admire her quiet strength, the way she still showed compassion even as she was broken down piece by piece. There is nothing romantic about what she lived through, but there is something sacred about her endurance. She was surviving in the middle of hell, keeping herself alive while the world around her kept collapsing. That kind of strength does not come from hope; it comes from something deeper, something primal. Her will to stay alive when there is no light left to follow and hope has faded really resonates with who she is.

READER'S REFLECTION:

1. When have you felt yourself slipping into a place that was hard to climb out of emotionally or mentally?
2. What early signs tell you that you're beginning to lose control or direction?
3. How do you usually cope when everything starts to feel overwhelming or chaotic?
4. Who or what helps you anchor yourself when your thoughts begin to spiral?
5. What does reaching out for help look like for you, and what holds you back from doing it sooner?

The Final Sequence of Events

I remember the day I went to pay the fee and filed for divorce. I was so happy! The divorce was finalized in mid-September 2013. That day in court, I had to agree to keep his last name, another form of his control, and pay him half of my thrift savings account. Even though I wasn't required to by law, I said I would agree to it if he would just let me go. At the age of forty-two, I was finally free and on my own for the first time. During the nine months the courts make you wait for your divorce date, I tried to start living a little.

I had been denied so much in my life. I had seen an advertisement for a local bikini contest. I had always wanted to model. That was my dream that he took away from me. I wasn't *allowed* to pursue that, and that modeling was for whores, and that I wasn't pretty enough. I decided it was time to start doing what I wanted, so I entered it. I didn't win, but I made friends with people who gave me opportunities to model. In October 2013, I made a new friend online through a mutual friend. I had done a photo shoot in a Native American-style bikini, my first one, I believe. People were making rude comments about the picture. My new friend came to my defense and stood up for me. We started talking through Messenger and were just friends. He was always there for me to talk to; it was nice to have a friend again.

My ex and I eventually had to move again; the rental owner wanted to move back into the farmhouse. I rented a small house just south of town. It was a small two-bedroom place. I told him that we should have separate bedrooms to convince the disability rep that we were no longer a couple. We were getting a divorce, but were living under the same roof for financial reasons. He went for it.

However, one night, he was arguing with me because he was angry that I wouldn't get him more beer before I went to work. He came into my room yelling at me and swung at me a few times. His disease was causing him to become imbalanced, and his health was rapidly deteriorating. I was able to move out of the way before he hit me. He wasn't as strong or as fast as he had been. I knew the stairs were difficult for him, so I decided to stay in the partially finished attic after that. I said it would be quieter for me to sleep for work.

One day, he was drunk and arguing with me again about wanting money and accusing me of cheating. I was making food for us before I had to go to work. He caught me off guard when he hit me in the head from behind. I was so outraged that I shoved him away from me. He staggered a bit and lost his balance. His balance wasn't good even when sober. I took a step back from him and ran up the stairs. I got ready for work, and before I left, I told him I was leaving him, and the divorce was going to be for real. I refuse to live like this anymore. He laughed at me in disbelief and said, "Go ahead and try to leave. You have nowhere to go and no money to leave. If you do, I will find you and kill you. You stupid Cunt. I have nothing left to lose, and I am dying anyway."

Over the next several months, I spent most of my time in the attic. I slept on a hardwood floor and worked two jobs, day and night, trying to keep bills paid and save up to move out and get away. We didn't speak much after that, except to get him a beer, demand money, or accuse me of something. He would argue with me whenever he could, so I would stay in the attic when I wasn't working. He now knew that I intended to leave him in the near future. I don't think he thought I would follow through with it or find a way to leave him. He would say to me, "Go ahead bitch, and try to leave me and see what happens." I told him that day that I was going to leave him or die trying. At that point, I didn't care what happened to me.

I woke up from a nap one day after working as a roofer and was walking out the door. He laughed and said, "Good luck getting to work, bitch!" I walked outside, and my car was gone. He sold it to the junkyard. He said, "I sent your car to the junkyard bitch, and am getting drunk with the money from it." I was absolutely shocked. How in the fuck was I supposed to get to work? I ended up calling a coworker and begging for a ride. I bummed rides to and from work for a while. I ended up buying a four-hundred-dollar beater to get me to and from work. Every day, I would try to work hard and stay away from him. I still paid for all the food, bills, and his medicine, etc. I was secretly buying things from the thrift store, hoping to save them for when I would be able to move out someday.

I still had no idea how I was going to get enough money to move out. I struggled to pay my bills because the IRS was garnishing my wages. The roofing company that he had put in my name all those years earlier had never paid taxes. He lied to me, saying he had taken care of it, to hide the fact that he hadn't paid them each year. After a few years, they garnished my wages, and I barely had any money left for myself. The IRS said I owed them $22,000. They had been garnishing my wages for several years now. I cried a lot. I didn't think I would ever get out. Several months passed, and I eventually spoke with a coworker about my situation. I couldn't get a loan on my own because he had destroyed my credit. My coworker agreed to co-sign a loan for me so I could get out. I cried so hard with relief. One step closer to freedom. A few weeks later, I found an apartment that would accept my fur babies. I couldn't move in until November, when the current tenants would vacate. I was keeping it a secret for my own safety.

One day, I was in the basement doing laundry, and he came down there and said, "So you think you are really going to leave me, huh?" I went upstairs today when you were gone and saw you had boxes packed. You really think you are going to fucking leave me?" He shoved me unexpectedly hard and hit me on the side of my face. He then pulled a kitchen knife and said, "You are not fucking leaving me, not alive! I always told you that if you ever tried to leave, I would kill you. You stupid Bitch, I have nothing to lose." He then lunged at me with the knife, attempting to stab me in the chest. Fortunately, due to his weakened condition, I dodged his attempt, getting only a small cut on my arm, and shoved him out of the way. Like any bad horror movie, I ran for the stairs in the attic. I needed to grab my stuff for work; he usually has a hard time making it up the steps. He staggered back a few steps, almost losing his balance. He was determined to make it up there to get me. A few minutes later, a can bag I had set on the door was making noise. I put that on the door to give me a warning when he was going to try to come up. He was shouting obscenities, and he managed to make it up the stairs. He still had the knife in his hand. I am pretty sure he had every intention of killing me, now that the reality of losing me had sunk in. He came walking towards me, still spewing slurs and threats.

At this point, my fight-or-flight response was kicking into overdrive. This was it. I had to do something. I grabbed my phone, and as he lunged at me once again, I was able to dodge past him and get down the stairs. I ran to my car, locked the doors, and called the cops. I sat in the car with the doors closed and locked, completely petrified. I didn't say anything about the knife and hid the small cut on my arm, just stated that he shoved me. I had never called the police or anyone else due to fear of what he would do after they left. He would always tell me that if I did, it would get so much worse when he got out.

I went back inside with the officers to get my work stuff. He was calling me a bitch and everything else in front of the officers. One of the officers took me into the kitchen to talk to me. The officer told me he would be going to jail for assaulting me, and my face had a red spot from him hitting me. They asked if I wanted a temporary restraining order from him, and I said yes. When he realized that he was going to jail, the real monster in him emerged. He screamed at the top of his lungs, "I can't believe you are doing this to me, you fucking bitch! You are going to pay for this! You think a fucking piece of paper will stop me?" I got so afraid that I told them to drop the restraining order. He went to jail, and I went to work.

The next morning, I called the rental company and asked if I could pick up the keys early. The apartment wouldn't be ready for a couple of weeks, as the painting and repairs weren't complete yet. I said I didn't care about that. I had an emergency going on. He got me the keys that day. Before and after work, I began moving things into the apartment. I moved my dog and two cats first, fearing that he would kill them when he got out. I didn't have much time between the two jobs, so I moved whatever I could over the weekend. Monday morning, I received a call from the police, and he was released that same morning. I WAS SO SCARED!

I packed my car with whatever else I could fit in, including the items I had bought and hidden. I got the hell out of there. I did not pack or take anything that we had gotten together. I didn't want anything that would remind me of him. It wasn't long before he started blowing up my cellphone. I answered it, and he immediately started screaming at me, "You are going to pay for this. Now I have a fine to pay because of you, you lying cunt!" I told him I didn't care what he thought. I was done and moving on with my life. I wished him well, but I was done.

My first night in my own place! I felt a great sense of relief and happiness! I was so delighted to be out and on my own. I was also so petrified that he would find me and keep his promise and kill me. I kept my car hidden in the garage. I had the landlord install deadbolts on the front and back doors. I was so happy to have my freedom and independence. I was perfectly fine with spending the rest of my life alone. At that time, I had become very good friends with the person who stood up for me when I wore a Native American-themed bikini. His name was Brad, and we talked every day. I didn't find the courage to meet him until the end of December 2013. We connected right away, eventually started dating, and have been a couple since.

My ex would call at all hours of the day. Sometimes to beg for me to come back, sometimes asking to get money from me, but almost always to threaten and belittle. I continued to pay for the rent, utilities, his medication, and other expenses. Despite how mean and verbally abusive he was. I had zero obligation to him. I owed that motherfucker nothing. I had given him everything, but I was always the responsible and kind-hearted person. I told him that I would help him until his disability was approved. He had no income. I would drop off food and keep his bills paid, all while paying my own bills.

He constantly harassed me daily until the point where I stopped answering his calls. After about four months, I told him I wouldn't be able to keep paying his rent. He would have to stay with a relative until he got his disability income or my thrift money, whichever comes first. I gave him thirty days' notice before I stopped paying. I told the landlord that I had moved out and would no longer be paying rent. One day, I dropped off the food and groceries he had requested. It was still winter, and he had all the windows and doors open, along with the thermostat set as high as it would go. I asked him what the fuck was going on. He said, "The bill is in your name, right bitch?!" I will make you pay in more ways than one!"

After that day, I just left his groceries outside the door. He eventually moved. The landlord called and said I would receive a bill for $5,000 worth of damages to the rental property. My ex had broken out several windows and screens. He punched holes in all the walls. He blatantly ran up a three-thousand-dollar heating bill. I was so pissed. That was the thanks I got for helping the piece of shit! At this point, because I was the only income, and he was on disability, all the creditors would come after me since they couldn't go after him. I could either agree to pay or face court action. Once again, I would be the one to pay the price for his evil ways and vindictiveness.

REFLECTION:

Absolute freedom came with costs. It is not clean, easy, or triumphant. Bonnie's came with fear, guilt, and years of damage that do not disappear just because the door finally closes. I still think about what it must have taken for her to walk away finally. It wasn't freedom that waited for her; it was exhaustion and silence. After years of fear, control, and pain, she somehow found enough strength left to stand up and go. I often wondered how she still showed compassion to the same man who destroyed her, paying his bills and bringing him food even after everything he had done. That kind of grace doesn't come from weakness. It comes from surviving too much and still choosing to be decent when he wasn't decent to her. I can't help but admire her strength. Her freedom didn't come clean or easy, but she earned every piece of it, and I don't think anyone can understand the gravity of that unless they've had to fight their way out too.

READER'S REFLECTION:

1. When you look back on moments of crisis or collapse, what finally made you decide it was time for change?
2. How do you process the ending of one chapter when you can't see what's next?
3. What emotions come up when you think about closure? Fear, peace, relief, or uncertainty?
4. Who or what reminded you that you were still worthy of hope even at your lowest point?
5. What lessons can only be learned when everything else has fallen apart?

The End

When he had his first stroke around 2012, the doctor said that with his diabetes, he must quit drinking, smoking, doing drugs, and start to take better care of himself, or he would be dead in two to five years. In 2014, I got a call from my former brother-in-law, saying that my ex had another stroke and was in the ICU in a coma. I found out that he had been in a coma for over 24 hours, and he wasn't expected to make it. His family asked me to visit them there. I told them I wasn't sure. I talked with my boyfriend and told him about it. I told him I wasn't sure if I wanted to go to the ICU and see him or not. He was very supportive and said that he would understand if I needed to say goodbye. I said I was going to go, but I decided against it. When I sat back and thought about it, in my heart, I didn't want to see him. He didn't deserve a visit from me. He was no longer part of my life, and I refused to let him back in any way. So, I decided not to go.

I later found out that he was in a coma for three days and woke up. He was hospitalized for two weeks, and my own brother sat up there by him, knowing all too well what he had done to me. The brother that I took into my home, and he witnessed some of my abuse. I was so glad that I didn't go. Once he was out of the ICU, the harassment continued. Someone eventually showed him a picture of my boyfriend on Facebook. He stopped harassing me as much; only on occasion did he, knowing my boyfriend would protect me.

My boyfriend and I eventually moved in together in July of 2015. One day, shortly after that, his car was keyed all the way down the driver's side. I am almost positive it was my ex-husband. I was worried he was going to leave me because of the harassment. We discussed it like normal people do, and he said he would get it fixed and move on. We ended up installing Ring cameras after that happened, just in case we needed to capture anything. The harassment lessened as my boyfriend and I began our lives together. My pain and suffering were finally lessening. We were a great couple and thoroughly enjoyed being together. I was finally finding out what life was supposed to be like. How true love was supposed to feel. How a man honestly treats a woman he loves. All my life, I had no idea how good it feels.

My ex died in his sleep on August 1st, 2015, due to a massive stroke and heart attack. I guess his body wasn't discovered for three days. The day I got the phone call, I was so sad for the family and his daughter, but inside I felt relief in my heart and soul. Relief that I didn't have to live in fear anymore. I didn't have to look over my shoulder at the grocery store constantly, worry about walking to my car in the parking lot at work, or anywhere else for that matter.

I did go to the funeral to be supportive of his daughter and his siblings. Two years later, his daughter died from an overdose of fentanyl laced heroin. Eventually, the nightmares that I had every night slowly stopped. Whenever I had a nightmare, my boyfriend would wake me up, hold me tight, and talk to me. I eventually married him. I have never been happier in my life. This is how life and love are supposed to be. I have deep scars that will never go away, but today I stand as a strong, free, and independent survivor and have learned to love again. I am learning to have self-esteem and to love myself. My husband has helped me stay strong and heal so much.

At first, I wasn't sure whether I wanted to write my story. I was leaning towards saying no thanks. I did not want to relive the pain and bring it back into my thoughts. I didn't want to trigger nightmares once again. I put my past in a box and stuffed it away. I live a happy life filled with love, surrounded by a husband who is loving and supportive. My husband and I discussed this, and perhaps sharing my story might help me in some way. I am not sure, but the main reason I decided to tell my story was that if I could help just one person get out of a bad situation, it would be worth reliving my nightmare. Maybe, just maybe, I will be helped through this process. This storytelling process has been a lot harder on me than I thought it would. This whole ordeal has been painful and draining, and many tears have fallen. It's been a process. I still have triggers that will give me anxiety, panic attacks, nightmares, or fits of crying. This story is a fraction of living almost thirty years of hell. Mostly, I am a strong and happy survivor. I am me, finally! I will be forty-eight in May of 2019. Forty-eight! I feel cheated out of the twenty-seven years my ex stole from me. I am proud of how far I have come and who I am today. I AM A SURVIVOR!

I want to thank my husband, Brad, for all his endless support and love. Always helping me heal and encouraging me to do what I want. It is not easy to love someone who has lived through this kind of trauma. He is amazing. Thank you for being my rock!

Many will ask me why I didn't leave sooner. I was afraid my ex-husband would find me and kill me. I was scared he would kill my pets. He made it hard for me to leave. I had no place to go, no way out, and no resources. It took me hitting rock bottom. It took me getting so low and miserable that I wanted to end it all. I was either going to get away or die trying. I honestly didn't care which. My way out of him was his getting sick and weaker; otherwise, I am sure he would have killed me. Then, no one would have the opportunity to hear my story. I am a survivor, and hopefully someone else can be too.

Bonnie's story is more than a memory. It is a testament to survival. Across these chapters, she shared her pain, her losses, and the long road back to herself. The courage it takes to relive those years in words cannot be overstated. Every chapter reopened an old wound but also healed another scar. Through her story, she found her voice again and permitted others to find theirs. There were years of silence, moments of fear, and times when walking away seemed impossible. She did it anyway. That kind of strength does not appear overnight. It grows from every tear shed, every prayer whispered, and every decision to keep going when giving up would have been easier.

For anyone who has lived a version of Bonnie's story, know this: what happened to you does not define who you are, and you are never alone in your healing. The road out of trauma is never quick or straightforward. Each step forward is a declaration that your life belongs to you again. Her courage reminds us that even in the darkest places, light still waits to be seen. Love, trust, and forgiveness do not erase the past. They transform it into strength.

This is the end of Bonnie's story, but not the end of her journey. Her voice lives here to remember what she endured and to show what survival looks like in its raw and honest form. It stands as proof that healing is possible, that peace can be earned, and that those who were once broken can become the very ones who help others rebuild.

REFLECTION:

Our stories started to intertwine, and what permeates most is not just what she endured but how she kept going. She lived through years of fear, isolation, and survival, yet somehow, she never lost her capacity for empathy. Even after everything he took from her, she still showed compassion when she could have chosen hate. That kind of resilience is rare. It does not come from strength alone; it comes from a spirit that refuses to die. I see her story as both a warning and a promise. A warning of what cruelty can do, but a promise of what courage can become. She faced every darkness and still reached for light. That is something most people will never understand until they have lived it.

Today, I see what survival can grow into when it is finally met with peace. I was the person who stood beside her when the nightmares still lingered, when trust was fragile, and when love felt like a risk. Watching her heal taught me that love is not about rescuing someone. It is about standing still while they learn to feel safe again and allowing themselves to heal. Our life together is proof that even the most broken people can become something whole. The past will always be part of her story, but now it lives beside something better for us in quiet mornings, laughter, and the kind of safety that cannot be taken away. This is where her story and mine became one. This is where survival becomes living.

READER'S REFLECTION:

1. When you reach the end of a painful journey, what helps you recognize that it's truly over?
2. How do you find peace when closure doesn't come in the way you hoped?
3. What parts of you have changed because of what you've survived?
4. How can endings become the soil for new beginnings instead of just reminders of loss?
5. What does it mean to you to walk away from something while still holding compassion for yourself and others?

Please note: If you have experienced or are currently experiencing abuse, know that you are not alone. Help is available. In the United States, you can call the National Domestic Violence Hotline at 1-800-799-SAFE (7233) or visit thehotline .org for confidential, 24/7 support. If you are outside the U.S., please look for local hotlines and resources in your country. You deserve safety, healing, and a life free from abuse.

III

Conclusion

The Beauty of Not Being Normal

When I reflect on everything that brought me here, I see a road lined with wreckage and hope. Some nights felt endless, and mornings that arrived too soon, moments when I swore I was done, and others when something unseen kept me moving. I did not rise out of comfort. I grew out of pain. Every scar, every broken piece, every loss became part of the foundation that steadied me when I finally stood on my own. Bonnie's story reminded me of that truth in a way few things ever have. Her courage to tell the untellable mirrored my own search for meaning inside the mess. Together, our stories became proof that healing is not a single moment of light but a long walk through the dark with faith that dawn will come. I used to think survival meant holding everything together. Now I know it means allowing myself to fall apart, to rebuild, and to keep walking anyway. This journey has never been perfect, but it has been real. And real is what saved me.

Survival is about refusing to give up.

I used to chase the idea of normal like it was a finish line I could reach if I just worked harder, loved better, or fixed myself fast enough. But normal was never real. It was a word that covered up pain, pretended everything was fine, and kept me silent when I needed to scream. What I finally understand is that being normal only means living by someone else's definition of enough. It leaves no room for the scars that shaped you or the strength it took to keep going. The beauty of not being normal is that it frees you to stop pretending. It lets you stand in the truth of who you are and find peace in your own story. When I let go of what the world expected, I found authenticity. The kind of honesty that feels uncomfortable at first but eventually becomes the only way to live. Normal was never the goal. Becoming whole was.

Normal is an illusion.

Somewhere along the way, I realized that the details of our stories might differ, but the ache underneath them feels the same. Pain may wear a thousand faces, but it always asks the same question: Will you rise again? I have met people who lost everything and somehow kept their kindness, and others who carried invisible battles no one could see. It made me understand that survival is not a competition. It is a quiet promise we make to ourselves to keep showing up even when it hurts. Bonnie and I found our strength in different ways, but both paths led to the same truth. Healing is not about erasing the past. It is about learning to live beside it without letting it own us. Every person who picks up this book is carrying something heavy, and I hope that these words help you set it down, even for a moment. None of us were meant to be perfect. We were meant to be real, and that is enough.

Real is the only thing that matters.

I learned that healing doesn't mean fixing everything. It means facing what you can, and letting go of what you cannot. It means controlling the controllables — your effort, your honesty, your choices — and forgiving yourself for the rest. Progress is not perfection. It is persistence. Every time you rise again, you prove that your story is still unfolding. I once thought strength meant never needing help. Now I see that real strength lives in those who keep trying, who stay humble, and who never stop learning. Love, real love, is built on truth, patience, and shared effort. It does not rescue you. It reminds you that you are worth saving.

Love is not the reward for healing. It is the reason we keep trying.

Every story has a purpose, even the ones we wish had never happened. When we tell our stories, we allow others to face theirs. That is why this book does not end here. It is meant to keep going through every person who has lived through darkness and still found their way toward the light. If something in these pages reminded you of your own story, I hope you share it. Speak it. Write it. Let it breathe. Your truth matters more than you think. The silence that once protected you no longer serves you. There is strength in breaking it. That is why I created the No One Is Normal podcast, a place where real people can share what they have survived, what they have learned, and what they are still fighting to understand. Every story told there becomes a bridge for someone else to cross. If you have a story worth sharing, I want to hear it. The world needs your voice as much as you need someone to listen.

Stories silence the noise and heal the wounds.

As I reach the end of this story, I am reminded that survival is not the same as living. It took me years to understand that healing is not a destination but a decision I have to make every single day. There will always be scars, but scars mean that something tried to break you and failed. They are proof that you endured. When I look at where we are now, I see two people who refused to let pain define them. We did not escape untouched, but we walked through the fire and found each other on the other side. That is the beauty of starting again. Life does not hand you a clean slate. It gives you a second chance, and what you create from it becomes your legacy.

Every new beginning is the doorway back to yourself.

If you take anything from this book, let it be this. You are not alone. You are not broken. You never were. You are still changing, still healing, and still finding your way. You were never meant to be normal. You were meant to be real — raw, human, and whole in your own way. The world does not need a perfect version of you. It requires the one who is still trying, still learning, and still showing up. The beauty of not being normal is that it frees you to be human. It reminds you that your story, no matter how messy or painful, still has meaning. You are still here, and that means there is more to write.

You were never meant to be normal.

You were meant to be you.

Afterword

Writing this book was more than storytelling. It was an act of emotional release for me. For a long time, the things I carried sat too heavy to talk about out loud without choking up or feeling inadequate. Putting them on paper let me breathe again. The process pulled the pain, confusion, and lessons out of my head and gave them shape. It gave me something I could look at, understand, and finally set down. What started as turmoil became clarity. What began as shame turned into something close to peace.

No One Is Normal wasn't written to offer advice or perfection. It was written to be honest. It was about the mistakes, the dark places, and the moments of blessings that showed up when I least deserved them. If even one reader finds their own story somewhere in these pages, then the purpose was met.

The upcoming *No One Is Normal* podcast will continue this conversation. It's a place for real stories like mine, Bonnie's, and others to be told without filters or judgment. Because being human isn't about fitting in, it's about being seen, heard, and accepted precisely as we are.

Thank you for reading.

And if you've ever felt like you were the only one who didn't fit, you're not alone. You never were.

To stay connected or share your own story, visit *www.bradhhill.com* or follow the *No One Is Normal* podcast. The conversation continues there. Raw, honest, and ongoing.

— **Brad H. Hill**

About the Author

Brad H. Hill is the primary voice behind *No One Is Normal*. Bonnie Hill brings her own voice and perspective, adding heart and honesty through her story of survival, resilience, and rediscovery. Together, they write from lived experience and from trauma and addiction to healing and rebuilding. Their work is grounded in truth, vulnerability, and the belief that even in the darkest places, light can still be found.

Brad writes with unfiltered intensity, shaped by a lifetime of reflection, loss, and transformation. His words carry the grit of someone who has rebuilt himself piece by piece. Bonnie's presence anchors the book with compassion and strength, offering the emotional clarity that comes only from walking through the flames and surviving.

Together, they dismantle shame, challenge the illusion of normal, and remind others that healing is not only possible. It's powerful. *No One Is Normal* is more than a story. It's a reminder that survival is not the end of the journey; it's where the real story begins.

You can connect with me on:

🌐 https://www.bradhhill.com

🐦 https://x.com/BHill81135

📘 https://www.facebook.com/profile.php?id=61582270002096